ANTI-AGEING
EXOTIC BLENDS

Minnie Pandit
Dr. Amitabh Pandit

An imprint of
B. Jain Publishers (P) Ltd.
USA - EUROPE - INDIA
www.bjainbooks.com

ANTI-AGEING EXOTIC BLENDS

First Edition: 2008
2nd Impression: 2010

All rights reserved. No part of this book may be reproduced, stored in a retrieval system or transmitted, in any form or by any means, mechanical, photocopying, recording or otherwise, without any prior written permission of the publisher.

© with the authors

Published by Kuldeep Jain for

HEALTH HARMONY

An imprint of
B. Jain Publishers (P) Ltd.
An ISO 9001 : 2000 certified Company
1921, Street No. 10, Chuna Mandi,
Paharganj, New Delhi 110 055 (INDIA)
Phones: 91-11-2358 0800, 2358 1100, 2358 1300, 2358 3100
Fax: 91-11-2358 0471 | Email: info@bjain.com
Website: www.bjainbooks.com

Cover design & layout: Vijesh Chahal

Printed in India by
J.J. Offset Printers

ISBN: 978-81-319-0278-3

DEDICATION

SALUTATIONS TO OUR LORD SHIRDI SAI BABA.
HE WHO IS OUR ALL IN ALL – OUR UNIVERSE

This work is inspired by him, caused to be written by him, to reach out to millions, only by him.

Seeing him in all, this work is offered to the readers to use, utilise, grow, learn and use the truths of natural law to become what is their absolute potential.

May our Lord Sai Baba Bless us all.

ACKNOWLEDGEMENTS

We would like to express our heartfelt gratitude to the members of our extended family: Kalsis, Agarwals, Bedis, Gidwanis, Prakashs, Khans and the Balanis of Lucknow.

Special reference is to be given to both our Photographers: Mr. Yogesh Aditya and Mr. Brijesh Bhatia for their full co-operation, flexibility and top professionalism. They have indeed given the colors to our book.

PUBLISHER'S NOTE

It is a great pleasure to publish this work on anti-ageing drinks. Today, when the markets are loaded with recipe books, the thought is very clear in the air that people want something which is tasty as well as healthy. Dr. Amitabh Pandit who is an expert in Orthomelecular science and Minnie Pandit who is the introducer of the living food cuisine and creator of recipes produced by Saidas Healing Foundation have put their knowledge & expertise to bring out these wonderful anti-ageing drinks which not only slow down the process of ageing but are rejuvenating and revitalising as well.

Orthomolecular science emphasizes the ingredients to be taken in a form which is absorbable by the body & to get the maximum benefit from it. The idea is to use the foods in the form they should be absorbable. Go ahead and enjoy these tasty, delicious, invigorating drinks and feel young and healthy. We will be happy to receive the readers' comments and suggestions for this work.

– Kuldeep Jain
CEO, B. Jain Publishers (P) Ltd.

INTERNATIONAL NAMES

English	Hindustani	Spanish
SPICES		
Bay leaf	Tej patta	Hoja de cala
Bishop's weed	Ajwain	----
Black cumin seeds	Jeera	Alcaravea
Black peppercorn	Kali mirch	Pimienta negra
Caraway seeds	Shahi jeera	Comino
Cinnamon	Dalchini	Canela
Cloves	Laung	Clavos
Coriander seeds	Dhania sookha	Semillas de cilantro
Dry Ginger	Sounth	Jengibre seco
Fennel seeds	Saunf	Regaliz
Fenugreek	Methi	Fenogreco
Ginger	Adrak	Jengibre
Green cardamom	Hari elaichi (choti elaichi)	----
Liquorice	Mulathi	Hinojo
Nutmeg	Jaiphal	Nuez moscada
Poppy seeds	Khus khus	Semillas de amapola
Saffron	Kesar	Azafrán
Turmeric	Haldi	Cúrcuma
Vanilla Bean	Vaneela	----

English	Hindustani	Spanish
HERBS		
Chamomile	Chamomile	Manzanilla
Coriander leaves	Hara dhania	Hojas de cilantro
Curry leaves	Meethi neem patti	Hojas de crurry
French mint	Hara poodina	Menta francesa
Holy basil	Tulsi	Albahaca
Lemon grass	Gaudhatrana	Hierbas del árbol de limón
Lemon verbena leaves	Lemon verbena Patti	Hojas de limón
Oregano	Origano Patti	----
Parsley	Prajmoda	Perejil
Red hibiscus flower	Chinese rose	Rosa china
Rosemary leaves	Rosemary Patti	Romero
Sage	Saij Patti	----
Spearmint	Spearmint	Hierbabuena
Sweet basil	Niazbo	Albahaca dulce
Tarragon	Tarragon	Tarragona
Thyme	Thyme	Tomillo

English	Hindustani	Spanish
ASSORTED INGREDIENTS		
Almonds	Badam	Almendras
Apple	Seb	Manzanas
Barley	Jaun	Cebada
Black currant	Kali kishmish	Pasas negras
Black salt	Kala namak	Sal negra
Celery	Ajwain ka patta	Apio
Corn silk	Makke ka bal	Maíz
Dry apricots	Sookhi khumani	Chabacanos secos
Eucalyptus leaves	Safeda ke patte	Hojas de eucalipto
Figs	Anjeer	Higos
Haritaki	Harad	----
Indian Gooseberry	Amla	Grosella hindú
Java plum	Jamun	Manzana roja
Lemon rind	Nimboo ka chilka	Cáscara de limón
Munakka	Munakka	----
Orange juice	Santre ka ras	----
Orange rind	Santre ka chilka	Cáscara de naranja
Prunes (European)	Meetha sookha aloobukhara	Ciruelas
Radish leaves	Mooli ke patte	Hojas de rábano
Raisins	Kishmish	Pasas
Red skin potato	Lal aloo	Papa de piel roja
Rose hips	Gulab ka phal	Rosas
Rose petals	Gulab patti	Pétalos de rosa
Sultanas	Sundekhani kishmish	Sultanas
Turkish apricots	Turkey kee khumani	Chabacanos turcos
Wheat sprouts	Ankurit gehun	Trigo entero
SWEETENERS		
Honey	Shahad	Miel
Maple Syrup	Maple Syrup	Miel de maple
Dates	Khajoor	Dátiles
Rock candy	Misri	Azúcar
Jaggery	Gud	----
Palm Candy	Taal misri	----

Authors' Note :

Human being is a living species and the body follows a natural process to keep a man alive. All our internal organs – heart, kidneys, liver, and intestines function efficiently, longer and smoothly when naturally grown foods with natural chemicals or living enzymes are given to them. Our life force is in the extract of natural foods.

The modern way of life is very harassing for the human body system and every one needs to realize the facts about nutrition, be it a man, a woman or a child. It is the food, which makes the body healthy, wealthy and wise.

The leisure and luxury is abandoned as soon as one part of the body system manifests its incapability to bear the atrocities of an indiscriminate lifestyle. It is better not to allow the crisis to reach an extreme and then transform. Let's promise today to give time and thought to our precious treasure of health. Let's vow right at this moment that we shall restore our life energy and retard our age.

A motherly and loving message to you all.

- Live with Nature
- Live by Nature
- Live for Nature

The exotic drinks in this book are to vitalize your youth and promote health multi-dimensionally – physical, mental, emotional and thus, allow happiness to prevail within.

– MINNIE PANDIT

What is it that you drink on a daily basis?

Is it tea, coffee, carbonated drinks or sherbets?

Your drink of the day plays a large role in keeping you fit. It is the fluid which bathes the cells of your body. It nourishes them and provides them food to live. Man drinks for a number of reasons. He drinks to quench his thirst, due to a habit, as a lifestyle or an addiction.

It is the changing of your drink and the reason behind it that can transform your life.

Your lifestyle can include numerous options of exotic drinks made at home with incredibly powerful ingredients capable of keeping your youthful looks, giving you high immunity and energizing your day.

DRINK for your health.

Let each and every morsel and sip that you take go to nourish your body.

– DR. AMITABH PANDIT

FOREWORD

Dr Amitabh Pandit and Mrs Minnie Pandit, a son and mother team's name is synonymous with wholesome living. They impress you by their exceptional insight into things healthy for you. Guided by an astonishing measure of the naturalist intelligence, they provide an instantaneous natural mantra to every health problem imaginable. They are the exceptional people you rarely meet in a lifetime.

They know the very secret of all the ways of living with good health while enjoying the most delicious assembly of all kinds of natural foods and drinks, mixed in the exact proportion, according to your personalised needs at any point in time. Thanks to the partnership of this amazing mother and son team, the food and the drink preparations are so delicious, you can hardly believe they can energise and uplift your mood, calm your nerves, improve immunity, cleanse you and even cure you permanently of the most awful of diseases.

At 74, my father who co-founded with my mother the world's largest school (www.cmseducation.org) works harder than any youth of 19. Instead of slowing down, he has been working with renewed vigour, enjoying every moment at the same time as living a tranquil life despite all the stress of managing a large institution. This is all thanks to Amitabh and Minnie Pandit's magic with natural food balances, weekly menu that my father, Jagdish Gandhi, lives by.

Isn't disease due to the disturbance in the balance, the proportionate equilibrium of all those elements of which the human body is composed, each component being present in a prescribed measure essential for maintaining the equilibrium of the whole? So as long as the constituent elements remain in their due proportion, there will be no physical cause for the incursion of the disease itself.

It is true if we want healthful living for all, "We must develop the science of medicine to such a high degree that they will heal illnesses by means of foods." (The Bahai Writings)

Minnie and Amitabh Pandit are jointly one such unique team which can unlock the gates of wisdom on this issue; a couple of incredible naturalist scientists if you will, who are modifying the way we think about health and nature.

Their new book is a treasure house of the finest of healthy drinks we can imagine. They all have a purpose: stimulating, calming, therapeutic or energising. Each sip has a vigour of its own and a healing power. I never imagined so many drinks could be derived from the world of nature, be so very delicious, and so very gratifying both to the eye and the body, thanks' to Minnie Pandit's powerful recipes.

The bounty of good health is the greatest of all gifts. Enjoy and savour this book, an invitation to the senses and more…

- Dr Sunita Gandhi, *Ph.D., Cambridge University*

RECIPE - Rx

Once in the morning, empty stomach as a substitute of bed tea.

In the evening if you feel the desire for it.

Thrice a day to derive therapeutic benefits

Note :
All the ingredients that go to make these exotic blends have been researched extensively for their nutritional content with their ability to heal. Readers are advised to take the counsel of a trained Orthomolecular practitioner qualified to diagnose and treat any ailment after fully assessing the individual medical history and personal body make up.
The contents of this book do not serve as a medical prescription.

INTRODUCTION

Orthomolecular view on natural foods versus processed foods:

Natural foods help your body's organs to secrete their respective enzymes allowing them to function in a natural manner.

The exotic blends have a marvellous healing capacity and provide wholesome benefits from the natural kitchen ingredients.

They are low in cost and very simple to make, giving us vibrant health and suffusing energy in our lives.

Just implement a life-style with your mind, set towards LIVING FOODS and turn away from the processed ones.

CONTENTS

Anti-ageing - A Reality Now	1
Fountain of Youth	3
The Spice of Life	7
Herbs for the Connoisseur	12
An Assortment of Ingredients	18
Sweeten Your Life	23
Exotic Blends	27
A – Z of Blends	126
Glossary	131
Bibliography	132

CHAPTER 1
ANTI-AGEING
A Reality Now

ANTI-AGEING - A REALITY NOW

Are you aged between 30 – 50 and yet feel that you are over the hill? Do you find your energy getting sapped and feel that the day has taken a toll on your health? Do you find your work stress to be excessive and that you have to drag yourself through the day? Do you feel that earlier you could work tirelessly and now with time, your body capacity to work, has taken a dip?

Our external capacities are dependent on our inner health and wellness. It is the functioning capacity of our organs which determines our strength and stamina.

Due to the living process going on inside the body there is continuous wear and tear of old cells which are replaced by new ones. This divine process is evident externally when the hair and nails which although cut regularly grow back gradually. The same process can be seen again in case of an injury or a wound. New and fresh skin is formed and the injured is shed off.

This internal process called metabolism ensures that our body is remade periodically. The average age of each cell varies from 3 days to 5 years. These cells in an average person are short lived and last from 3 days to maximum 2 years. The miracle is that this time span can be extended using the latest researched information discovered by orthomolecular science.

This futuristic life science has discovered ways to affect and alter the chemistry of the body at microscopic level, which is the cell structure and that too in a simple manner.

Orthomolecular science has found that the micronutrients entering the body through the food eaten, once digested go to make each and every part of the body.

It is the food and the combination in which it is taken that forms the very fabric of the body including blood, bones, nerves, organs, muscles and brain.

It is for this reason that orthomolecular science prescribes food in particular combinations. These combinations act synergistically to produce cells and tissues which last longer even up to 5 years.

As soon as the individual starts eating his food as prescribed, the transformation begins to take place. The body is flooded with micronutrients which it requires to regenerate and rebuild itself. As a result, over a period of time, the absolute chemistry of the body changes to produce fantastic levels of health and well being.

When this is adopted as a lifestyle – a rejuvenative effect is produced.

"Yes, we have a health plan: our coffee is made with chicken soup instead of water and the sprinkles on our donuts are antibiotics."

For instance, if a 35 year old person introduces such combinations and patterns in his dietary lifestyle. Each new cell being created in his body could have an average life of 5 years, and in next five years, his body would have rebuilt itself only ONCE as the cells have been replaced only once. As a result, even at the age of 50, this person will be experiencing the exuberant health that he would otherwise have enjoyed at the age of 38 years, since his biological structure has aged ONLY thrice in 15 years.

Orthomolecular science takes into consideration lifestyle factors like time schedules, work environment, traveling, socializing and hospitality.

It offers remarkable flexibility with little restrictions on quantity of food.

Its path breaking research has burst the previously held myths about calorie counting, dieting and the need to eat bland and boiled foods.

This anti-ageing life science is fast gripping the world by giving greater emphasis on creating well being and inner health. The external effects manifested are superior levels of energy, strength, stamina with greater flexibility and elasticity of muscles, skin suppleness, clearer thinking and cognitive ability with a vibrant glandular system.

This book introduces multiple options available for taking certain exotic blends according to the orthomolecular approach.

A health conscious reader would definitely be interested in knowing the advantages of the blends that he takes and also those that are good for his family including children. So be it spouse, mother, father or any other member of the family, one can go ahead and experience real rejuvenation.

CHAPTER 2
Fountain of Youth

Anti-ageing Exotic Blends

FOUNTAIN OF YOUTH

There are a number of drinks available in the market which claim to provide energy, health and vitality to the body.

All of these drinks are bottled or packed and have a shelf life for numerous months from the date of manufacture.

Let's bust this myth!!

Firstly, any drink made with natural ingredients and which has the potential to promote good health would not last on the shelf of a super market for such a long period of time. Natural extracts and products have an intrinsic quality of getting spoilt, fermenting and rotting after a specific time span as NATURE intended. This keeps the cycle of death and life continue with precision.

In nature anything old withers away to be replaced by the new. This law of NATURE is clearly evident in the growth of a tree. In Autumn the leaves of trees fall, which are replaced by fresh ones in Spring. Similarly fresh produce has a limited time frame during which it retains its nutrient content. Gradually, this is reduced and finally it wilts.

Every product having a shelf life of many months definitely contains chemicals and preservatives that have been added to it to prevent it from getting spoilt and unfit for consumption. Along with these artificial and synthetic preservatives there is a long list of chemicals that are put for flavoring, coloring and taste.

In addition, refined sugar is one of the major components of the so called health drinks that causes immense harm to the body. It will be prudent to take a look at the ingredients list of any drink that one picks up under the impression of it being an energy drink.

Apart from the health drinks, all the carbonated beverages are simply concoctions of sugar sweetened water and synthetic chemicals.

"You know we strongly discourage any sort of office romance. Someone heard you whisper 'I love you' to the cold drink vending machine."

Packaged soups that come with the 'add water and heat' instructions are least healthy as a warm drink. The consumer takes it alone or with a meal in the belief that he is taking 'Food' when in fact he is getting absolute zero nutrition.

Powdered, dehydrated vegetable extracts with preservatives do not provide any nutrition to the body. It cheats our body of its real requirement and at the same time adds elements which build up toxicity, deplete immunity reserves and cause it to malfunction.

These easy to prepare foods available under the garb of 'convenience' foods actually become the reason for considerable inconvenience in the form of ill health and malnutrition disorders.

Packed juices are the other category of drinks which people are guzzling by the gallons since it is advertised as a product having no artificial or synthetic flavor, no preservative and no added sugar.

It is the loop holes in laws governing edible products that allow such juices to be promoted in a manner giving incomplete information to the consumer. It keeps consumers in the dark about the reason , packed juices do not deteriorate in quality when kept for months.

The fact is that such juices have been ultra heat treated or pasteurized before they are packed. This process changes the entire chemistry of one of the finest foods that a man can take.

The minerals, vitamins and living enzymes are completely destroyed leaving only a fluid with sugar content behind.

This reality can easily be experienced by taking a glass of packed orange juice and comparing it with a glass of freshly extracted juice. The latter is wholesome, filling and provides vital ingredients to remain in optimal health.

Taking a daily cup of tea may be a religion for some, but a closer look at it may help change the mind completely.

According to the American Dietetic Association, on an average, a cup of tea contains 40mg of caffeine.

Caffeine like nicotine in tobacco is a dreadful poison, which causes gout and windy diseases. Excessive intake of tea or coffee increases the quantity of urine, which overloads the kidneys. A person addicted to tea passes urine three times more than a healthy person. But the toxic substance does not go out with urine rather it is solidified to form uric acid, which remains deposited in joints to cause gout and arthritis.

The red blobs are your red blood cells.
The white blobs are your white blood cells.
The brown blobs are tea. We need to talk.

Knock me out!!!

Tea leaf contains approximately 17% of tannic acid. Tannin is used in a tannery to make leather soft and shining. Tannin blocks the orifices of tiny cells in the body, which absorb nutrient from the food eaten. When tannin reaches the stomach it disturbs the secretion of juices primarily required for digestion of food. The consequence is indigestion and constipation further affecting the liver. Since tannin's effect is to dry up watery contents in the body, the skin also becomes rough and brittle. Its mental effect is similar to liquor or a narcotic drug, which gives a kick for a short duration and thereafter, gives rise to lethargy and listlessness. This prompts one to gulp another cup of tea to regain the earlier euphoria. It further leads to addiction and usually a person feels drowsy and morose on not getting his 'cuppa' for stimulation.

Anti-ageing blends

The world is opening up to a vast array of exotic infusions also called as teas, which are an invitation to the senses. These blends have anti ageing properties and are therapeutic in nature. Each one has a healing effect on body and mind.

Your cuppa – full of health: The early morning drink, before the day starts needs to be vibrant enough to awaken the entire being and to give the pep required to carry one through the day. An exotic blend chosen from amongst the ones described here just fit that bill. Each of the fusion buoys you up to higher planes of pleasure and brings with it a distinct after taste .They are potent and filled to the brim with antioxidants to give your body's immunity the boost it so requires in today's pacy life style.

Maximise true health benefits

1. Each and every infusion is healing and has a curative effect on the body .It would not make you addicted instead you would want to have it for health promoting benefits.
2. Each cup has an energizing impact. The ingredient be it spice, herb or sweetener has potent influence on the nerves bringing about a recharged feeling.
3. These energizing blends have an incredible variety of recognized nutrients as well as phytonutrient components. They are a rich source of minerals and vitamins that build your health sip by sip and keep you looking young for years to come.

These blends have multiple beneficial effects, with many of them being

- Stimulating
- Calming
- Energising
- Therapeutic

besides having properties of reducing the ageing process. These multiple effects make them suitable even for your children. They will love them!! To top it all, they do not get addicted to the regular tea or coffee habit.

The choices offered are multifold with each one giving variety in taste, flavor, benefit and most essentially the experience.

CHAPTER 3

The Spice of Life

Anti-ageing Exotic Blends

THE SPICE OF LIFE

Spices have long been the very essence of our foods. They have sent intrepid adventurers onto unknown oceans to find new places, people and trade routes. The Spice Route to China sucked in Marco Polo and brought the spice trade to Europe. Christopher Columbus set out to find the way to the source of spices and found the New World. The British Raj occupied India to gain its wealth, its spices and tea trade.

Spices even became a form of currency.

Spices are sacred, may be aphrodisiacs, make food tastier, and are filled with anti-oxidants.

It has been found by the US Department of Agriculture that spices have, ounce per ounce, measure for measure, more anti-oxidant compounds than fruits and vegetables.

Spice Ingredients

Cinnamon: This king of spice is the spice for heart.

1/2 teaspoon of Cinnamon every day can lower the level of cholesterol. It has an anti clogging effect on arteries and veins. Cinnamon relieves the pains of acute arthritis. It also inhibits bacterial growth in your stomach.

Liquorice: One of the most important medicinal herbs on the planet.

It has been used extensively in Chinese herbal medicine for thousands of years, in approximately half of their formulas.

Liquorice tends to improve the action of all the other herbs and has tremendous value in the reversal of auto-immune diseases.

Fenugreek: The seed of fenugreek is an effective nutritional supplement and has also been used by herbalists for many centuries for health benefits it provides.

This magic seed has the ability to aid the digestive process.

> **Lower your blood sugar by adding an infusion of fenugreek seeds to your early morning bed side ritual. Taking it in the morning and evening can keep the blood sugar in check.**

Are you diabetic? When taken with meals it is believed that fenugreek is able to slow down the rate at which sugar is absorbed into the body, whereby regulating blood sugar level. Fenugreek may induce or promote the production of insulin when blood sugar levels are elevated.

Clove: Your nutrient dense spice.

Clove's unique phytonutrient components are accompanied by an incredible variety of traditionally recognized nutrients, including omega fatty acids, calcium & magnesium. Cloves contain eugenol - an active component that prevents toxicity from environmental pollutants.

It displays anti-inflammatory activity by reducing inflammation of the joints and the digestive tract.

"Your cologne smells like spice. Oregano is a spice. Pizza is made with oregano. Some people like pizza with pepperoni. Pepperoni is made from pigs. As a vegetarian, that offends me. I'm filling a complaint against you!"

Bay leaf: The herb of heroes.
In ancient Greek and Rome, heroes were crowned with wreaths woven from bay leaves - and this is also from where we get the rather quirky phrase, 'resting on his laurels' !
Indian bay leaf has a rather different flavor.

- Bay leaf tea aids with therapy in migraines.
- It is useful for maintaining warmth in the body. Highly effective for cold.
- Its tea is excellent for digestion and will help those troubled with fermentation and gas in stomach and bowels.

Black cumin: For centuries, black cumin herb and oil have been used by millions of people in Asia, Middle East, and Africa to support their health.

This kitchen spice can raise respiratory health, stomach & intestinal health.

It increases blood circulation and supports the immune system.

The extract form is effective in regulating blood sugar levels, and stimulating bone marrow and immune cells.

Saffron: An aphrodisiac.

As a therapeutic plant saffron is considered an excellent stomach ailment remover and an antispasmodic. It helps in digestion and increases appetite.

Its synergistic blend is a boon for women since it regulates conception.

Greek mythology associates saffron with fertility and is considered an excellent stimulant.

Ginger/Dried Ginger/Thai Ginger: Ginger has been known for centuries in Asia for its healing powers. It is a proven anti-emetic, anti motion sickness remedy that surpasses even pharmaceutical drugs.

- Helps throat and prevents migraine headaches and arthritis.
- Is an antibiotic.
- Ginger has antidepressant, anti-diarrhoeal

and strong antioxidant activity.

This powerhouse of a spice surely knocks one down with its multiple benefits.

Peppercorn: Can keep you slim.

This powerful spice stimulates the taste buds in such a way that an alert is sent to the stomach to increase hydrochloric acid secretion, thereby improving digestion.

Black pepper promotes intestinal health by preventing the formation of intestinal gas.

This wonderful seasoning has an outer layer that stimulates the breakdown of fat cells, keeping you slim while giving energy to burn.

Cardamom: It is called the queen of spices and has been prized since ancient times. It was chewed by the Moghul emperors of India as a breath freshener, a tradition that still exists.

Key Benefits of Cardamom:
- Considered a key digestive and is used to treat stomach disorders.
- Helps to prevent vomiting due to its anti-spasmodic properties.
- Refreshes the breath and soothes the throat.

Bishop's Weed: The spice for women

Regular intake of this spice keeps the uterus healthy.

It is excellent for lactating mothers as it helps in production of milk. These seeds can enhance digestion, increase the appetite and control flatulence.

Take an exotic infusion containing Bishop's weed and feel the difference.

Nutmeg: It is also known as Myristica fragrans. The blend of nutmeg has the properties of healing rheumatism and muscle spasm.

It has the legendary ability of being an aphrodisiac.

Fennel Seeds: These seeds contain their own unique combination of phytonutrients.

It has extremely strong antioxidant potential with its volatile oil protecting the liver from toxic chemical injury.

Caraway Seeds: Its qualities were recognized by the ancient Egyptians, Greeks and Romans.

Caraway was said to prevent lovers from straying and thus, was once an essential ingredient in love potions.

The seeds of caraway were prescribed for bringing bloom to the cheeks of pale-faced young maidens.

The dried fruits or seeds, brown in color, are hard and sharp to touch. They have a pleasant odor, aromatic flavor, mildly sharp taste and leave a somewhat warm feeling in the mouth.

The caraway seeds, leaves and roots are considered useful in activating the glands. It is characterized as an excellent 'house cleaner' for the body.

Caraway seeds are useful in strengthening the function of stomach and counter possible adverse effects of medicines.

Coriander Seeds: They are dried after they ripen. They have an aromatic odor and an agreeable spicy taste.

The seeds contain both essential oil and fatty oils.

Coriander seeds reduce fever and promote a feeling of coolness.

The coriander blend helps lower blood cholesterol as it is a good diuretic and stimulates the kidneys.

Poppy Seeds: The white Poppy seeds are so small that a thousand of them would hardly weigh 0.3gm. Despite their size, stature and origin, they are highly nutritive.

They also exert a mildly sedative effect.

Turmeric: The Turmeric rhizome is aromatic, stimulant and a tonic.

This colorful spice is an excellent detoxifier for the body. It purifies the blood and cleanses the intestines of bacteria.

True wellness comes from good digestion and this spice tops the list in making that possible.

It corrects the disordered process of nutrition and restores normalcy in the digestive system.

Vanilla Bean: Is considered one of the most popular non-pungent spices – in fact it is one of the most widely used flavors in the world. History has witnessed Vanilla always being held with high regard, as it was a spice used by the Spanish royalty.

It has been considered as an aphrodisiac and was recommended by physicians to be drunk as an infusion or tincture for the purpose of raising male potency.

CHAPTER 4
Herbs for the Connoisseur

HERBS FOR THE CONNOISSEUR

The history of herbs is as long as the story of mankind, for people have used these plants since earliest times. Wars have been fought and land conquered for plants and even today we continue to depend on exotic species for many of our medicines and chemicals.

For a botanist, a herb is a plant that dies down to ground level at the end of the growing season while to a connoisseur it means a part of the plant that can be used as a blend.

Several herbs are important for the culinary herb garden. They posses volatile oils that are helpful in preventing wind formation or stimulating the secretion of digestive juices.

Most culinary herbs can be preserved by drying, but in most cases the fresh product has a better flavor. Herbs interact in complex ways with our body chemistry and their power to heal is formidable. Compared with synthetic drugs their action may seem very mild, but one should not underestimate the medicinal benefits of herbs.

Growing herbs in your own garden

A small herb garden can supply a wide range of organic, aromatic, edible and medicinal material for every day use.

How far to explore the treasure of herbs depends upon the space available and the type of climates and terrain enjoyed by the personal kitchen garden.

The indigenous forms have their real worth and effectiveness in teas, tonics and ointments, for their fragrance and for the complex flavors they impart to other foods. They are also easier to tend than most choice ornamentals.

A start can be made with essential culinary herbs, planted together in the vegetable garden. Later as the collection expands, the plants can be moved to a dedicated site elsewhere. Individual herbs may be tucked into existing beds and borders with other plants.

Whether the garden is a large expanse of soil and shrubs or a small front patch in front of a city house, herbs can be happily combined to produce an attractive display. Space is not a constraint for a garden of herbs.

Growing herbs in containers is the ideal solution where consideration of space, soil or climate suggests a plant might be difficult to grow.

Most herbs are adaptive to pots and other containers.

Herbs like mint can be grown simply by taking the root cuttings and planting them in trays, which can provide useful crops on a kitchen windowsill.

Herb growing is a practical choice for window boxes, balconies and roof gardens. It is easy to supply container- grown plants with the kind of soil they prefer and moving them under cover or to sunny spots if they are sensitive to cold or exposure.

Irrespective of the place where the herbs are grown – in pots inside the house or cultivated in a garden, immense pleasure is derived in cutting the fresh herbs to use personally or for guests and savoring the delights of aroma and taste in exotic anti ageing blends or cookery.

Herb Ingredients

1. Rosemary: Enhance your memory

Rosemary has a calming effect on the nerves and stimulates the circulation of blood, causing an increase in memory capacity.

Modern research has shown that rosemary contains substances that prevent the breakdown of neurotransmitters in the brain. So, if it's a child or an adult – a cup of Rosemary blend is the doctor's advice for greater memory power.

The big bonus with this herb is its effectiveness in combating hair loss, as it stimulates growth of hair follicles and promotes blood circulation in the scalp.

2. Parsley: This herb promotes optimal health. The activity of parsley's volatile oils qualifies it as a "chemo protective" food, and in particular, a food that can help neutralize particular types of carcinogens like cigarette smoke and charcoal grill smoke.

3. Curry Leaf: It improves the quality of digestive juices helping in digesting food better.

The smell and taste of curry leaves enhances the quality of the whole meal. Curry leaf blend promotes the action of the stomach and small intestine tackling multiple digestive problems caused by improper food intake.

4. Holy Basil: The leaves of holy basil are a nerve tonic and help sharpen memory. The holy basil blend is ideal for children during exams .These leaves also strengthen the stomach. Basil leaves are

> **Rosemary is an herb that can be used fresh or dried. It's flavour enhances the taste of the blend, brings a soothing and calming effect. This herb helps in stressed conditions and in depressive moods.**

regarded as an 'adaptogen' or anti-stress agent. Regular consumption of its blend provides significant protection against stress.

5. Lemon grass: It is the herb for children especially for their digestive problems. It reduces stomach cramps, brings down flatulence & colicky pain and even fever. The herb blend has an aroma that attracts the palate and gives a soothing sensation in the evening.

6. Mint: Mint has always been enjoyed for its wonderful aroma, great taste, and its healing power.

A soothing mint blend calms down the digestive tract and reduces the severity and length of stomach aches. Mint destroys the most harmful bacteria & fungi making the infusion a potent blend of pleasure and nutrition.

7. Red Hibiscus Flower: The hibiscus flower prevents cholesterol deposits in the arteries.

Its delightful infusion taken in the evening proves beneficial in preventing a number of cardiovascular diseases.

8. Thyme: Use thyme to offset ageing process.

The thyme herb has significant antioxidant capacity to protect the cellular membranes and is highly effective in delaying brain cells from ageing.

Thyme contains constituents which prevent microbial contamination. The essential oils in thyme decontaminate the intestines keeping them healthy and microbe free. Thyme being a nutrient rich herb, has a wide range of health supportive benefits, which can easily be availed by taking it in the form of a blend.

9. Chamomile: Traditionally used as a stewing herb, chamomile is popular since early Egyptian times. The herb blend is more famous for settling nervous disorders, stimulating the appetite and cleansing the blood. It is primarily the flowers, which are used after being collected and dried in the shade.

10. Lemon Verbena: It is a hearty herb with an unusually strong lemon scent and flavor to it.

Its leaves and flowering tops are used in teas.

It is your herb for anti-ageing as Lemon Verbena has the ability to help break

> **Thyme:** A small leaved herb and yet it vigors the digestive capacity in a big way. Keep fresh leaves handy in a muslin cloth or dried in a tight jar.

down cellulite, as well as to exert a soothing, healing and toning effect on the skin.

11. Tarragon: Tarragon fights fatigue and calms the nerves. It also promotes the production of bile by the liver, which aids in digestion and helps to speed the process of eliminating toxic waste from the body. Tarragon blend aids in this process.

12. Sage: This herb has been recommended by experts for about every known condition from snakebite to mental illness. Due to this, it has got the French name 'toute bonne' which means 'all is well'.

Sage guards against depletion of the brain's concentration of acetylcholine, a neurotransmitter crucial for brain functioning. It maintains the ability to think clearly even as one ages.

It reduces perspiration, fights against several infection causing bacteria, soothes pain from sore throat and tonsillitis and helps relax muscle spasms in the digestive tract.

13. Oregano: 'Delight of the Mountains' The ancient Greeks were the first to take advantage of this herb and termed it oreganos, meaning 'delight of the mountains'.

Oregano is prized for its strong flavor, pleasant aroma and also for its health benefits. It has proved more effective than commonly prescribed drugs for bacteria. It is a powerful source of many antioxidant vitamins assisting in slowing down the ageing process.

In fact, weight by weight oregano is considered to be one of the most antioxidant dense of all foods.

Herbs – All year round

For routine culinary purposes leaves and sprigs can be picked fresh as required and whenever available. However, many herbs are not evergreen or accessible round the year and it will be necessary at some point to gather them in larger quantities for preserving and subsequent storage for later use.

Drying the leaves and flowers: Living parts of plants contain large amount of water, as much as seven – eighths (7/8th) of their weight in many cases, and this must be removed before they can be safely stored.

In a warm and dry climate, leaves and flowers may be tied loosely together in small bundles and hung in an airy, dust free place away from the sun until they are brittle enough to break easily between the fingers (in dusty places enclose bundles in perforated bags) .They can also be spread on a table or shelf between sheets of news papers or muslin and turned daily or laid on a mesh screen that has been raised to allow air circulation beneath.

The aim is to retain most of the color, flavor and aroma of the original herbs. Bright sunlight and cold places should be avoided. Sunlight can bleach the color while cool conditions can increase the time taken for the herbs to dry resulting in loss of quality. In most cases a week's time should be long enough to dry the herbs.

Care is to be taken to keep each variety separate and the bags must be labeled clearly.

Rejuvenate your nervous system by sipping any lemon grass blend with lemon juice squeezed in it.

Steeping herbs to create a blend

The method of steeping an herb is to take the specified quantity of leaf such as mint or basil. The herb leaf could be fresh or dried as per the indicated recipe. These are then added to the teapot or jug and filled with boiling water.

The other ingredients may be boiled in the water prepared for steeping the herb.

Leave the infusion to steep for 5-8 minutes – allowing the herb oil and the essence of the leaves to get extracted into your blend. This would produce a fully flavored infusion that can then be strained through a sieve into your cup and relished.

CHAPTER 5
An Assortment of Ingredients

AN ASSORTMENT OF INGREDIENTS

Amla (Indian Gooseberry): "Amla is peerless among rejuvenative herbs."

- Ayurvedic text

- Rejuvenative - Amla nourishes all the body tissues and accelerates the cell regeneration process.
- Detoxify yourself - Amla helps in maintaining the health and functioning of the liver, allowing it to efficiently eliminate toxins from the body. Even accumulated toxins stored in the liver can be flushed out over time.
- Amla is a powerful food for the brain and it maximizes mental capacity.

Indian Gooseberry: They are available in the months of January to March. Pick the spotless Gooseberries for the use of eating or drinking. On keeping them they start to turn brown. At the time of using, sliver off those spots. The Indian Gooseberries are enormously regenerative and rejuvenative. It empowers the body to defend and protect itself from any incidence of disease. Restore your vital health by consuming them in season.

Apple & it's peel: They contain very potent antioxidants, which can even inhibit the growth of cancer cells. The natural sweetness of apple comes from its simple sugar fructose that helps to keep the blood sugar levels stable. The blend made from it has a sweetish fragrance that enhances the drinking experience.

Rose Petals: The blend ingredient for nerves.

Regarded as a mild sedative and antidepressant, the rose blend has a soothing effect on nerves and mind.

The essences in the rose flower have a positive influence on your entire well being.

Rose hips are an excellent source of vitamins A, B 3, C, D, and E. They also contain antioxidants like bioflavonoids and flavonoids.

Lemon and its Rind: Edmond Hillary, the man who conquered Mount Everest, said that the one thing that made it possible for him to reach the top was the lemon.

Lemons have a tangy flavor which adds taste to anything. The rind relieves flatulence, removes gastric discomfort & improves appetite.

Figs: This fruit helps in lowering high blood pressure and in improving bone density.

The mineral content of figs makes it a superb addition to the diet of women. They have a positive effect on weight management as well making it an ideal ingredient in a few of the exotic blends as given ahead.

Get remarkable healing effects and sweeten your early mornings or evenings with this fruit.

Raisins: These delicious dried grapes come in a variety of shapes & sizes. You have sultanas, black currants and munakkas. They are a top source of phytonutrients, which makes them a super rich antioxidant fruit. Raisins contain active ingredients to make better bones, healthy gums and teeth. For women concerned about preventing osteoporosis, adding raisins to their blend especially in the way detailed ahead would yield similar positive effects of oestrogen therapy in the most natural manner.

Haritaki(Terminalia Chebula): It is also called harad. It is a rejuvenative fruit originating in India. Harad forms an excellent remedy for the intestines and tones them up. It is also a laxative and has astringent properties.

Apricots: They are an excellent source of vitamin A, a nutrient essential for good vision. They contain antioxidants beta carotene and lycopene. Apricots are rich in a soluble fiber that lowers LDL cholesterol.

These fruits are deliciously healthy and uplift the BLEND they are added to.

Corn Silk: It is also called maize silk. It is a highly effective remedy for various ailments. Its therapeutic properties have made it very popular for keeping kidneys healthy.

Men with prostate disorders and women having water retention can take the corn silk blend with advantage.

This exotic blend aids in reducing obesity as well.

Red Skin Potato: Potato is a vegetable par excellence for its anti-ageing properties. It contains a variety of phytonutrients that have antioxidant activity. Vitamin B6 in potato is essential for the formation of virtually all new cells in the body.

Barley: This robust cereal's claim to nutritional fame is based on its being a very good source of fiber and selenium, and a good source of phosphorus, copper and manganese. It provides essential components for several major metabolic pathways, including thyroid hormone metabolism, antioxidant defense systems, and immune function.

> **Add to your daily food pattern, Apricots- to energize your vital organs with the required Minerals and Vitamins.**

Celery: A vegetable rich in vitamin C along with several active compounds that promote health.

These components support your immune system and at the same time relax the muscles around the arteries. It keeps blood flow in the body strong and heart healthy.

This potassium and sodium rich powerhouse regulates the fluid balance in the body.

Germinated Wheat: Wheat germ, the heart of the wheat kernel, is packed with protein, fiber, polyunsaturated fat, vitamins, and minerals. It's the most nutritionally dense part of wheat kernel, which also includes the endosperm and bran or outer husk. This is multiplied in the sprouted wheat.

Almonds: A high-fat food good for health!

That's the magic of almonds. It's content of health enhancing fats are associated with better functioning of the brain, more flexibility and longer lasting mobility of the joints.

The antioxidant action of vitamin E found in almonds and the magnesium provide double-barreled protection against diabetes and cardiovascular disease.

Prunes: Prunes are the dried plums. The high content of phytonutrients in prunes neutralizes oxygen-based damage to all our cell membranes and brain cells.

This prevention of free radical damage provides protection from a variety of disorders including atherosclerosis, diabetic heart disease, and colon cancer.

The potassium found in prunes also strengthens bones.

Radish Leaves: Leaves of the common vegetable radish contain more calcium, phosphorus, vitamin C and protein than radish itself.

They have a pungent flavor and its blend has tremendous effect on the liver. They stimulate the appetite and promote a healthy bloodstream.

Eucalyptus Leaves: The eucalyptus leaf has antibacterial, antifungal, antiseptic and antiviral qualities. It aids in decongesting and stimulating the circulation of blood.

The primary chemical constituent of eucalyptus is its essential oil.

The number of ready-made preparations that contain eucalyptus oil is enormous which shows its potential healing capacity. Every kind of product is represented, from pure oil through oil-containing ointments and rubs to candies and syrups.

CHAPTER 6
Sweeten Your Life

SWEETEN YOUR LIFE

Who doesn't have a sweet tooth?

Each one of us would like to have sweet –be it after meals, in between or before.

Our body runs and requires sugar to function at optimal levels of health and fitness.

Some of us may opt for artificial sweeteners in our dietary patterns. People often take them considering them to be safer than sugar.

However latest research shows the reality:

- They have harmful effects on the body's glandular system.
- Chemicals in them burden the excretory system.
- They can cause a variety of symptoms including headaches, severe depression, decreased vision, irritability, palpitations, burning and increased urination, joint pains and anxiety attacks.

Going beyond sugar: Sugar available in the market is a highly refined product unlike what Mother Nature intended for our bodies. It has an imbalancing effect on metabolism causing fatigue, sugar highs or dips, gain in weight and even aggravations of psychological kinds.

A high sugar intake is neither recommended nor desired by most of us and one is always looking out for healthier and safer options.

Natural sweeteners come in as a welcome change in this scenario and offer us wholesome, synergistic nutrition, enhanced metabolism and therapeutic benefits.

Dates: These are the 'crown of sweets'. Dates are an ideal food which is easy to digest. Within half – an - hour of taking them, the tired body regains a renewed vigor. They contain oil, calcium, sulphur, iron, potassium, phosphorous, manganese, copper and magnesium. In other words, one date is a minimum of a balanced and healthy diet.

Dates for women: Dates contain stimulants which strengthen the muscles of the uterus. On one hand this helps the dilation of the uterus at the time of delivery and on the other it reduces the loss of excessive blood after delivery. It is the best food for women in confinement and those who are breast-feeding their young ones. This is primarily because dates contain elements that assist in alleviating depression in mothers and enriching the breast-milk with all the elements needed to make the child healthy and resistant to disease. Prophet Mohammed had emphasized the importance of dates and their effectiveness in the growth of foetus.

Dates for men: In the early years, dates served as food for Muslim warriors. They used to carry them in special bags hung at their sides. They are the best stimulant for muscles and men of all ages can consume them to increase their muscular capacity and stamina.

Dates for children: Modern dietary authority patterns recommend dates for children suffering from a nervous nature or hyperactivity.

Dates, due to their rich calcium content help in strengthening the bones. Calcium deficiency in adults weakens the bones, making them brittle and among children causes rickets. These natural sweeteners counter such effects.

Maple syrup: Maple syrup is sweet - and we're not just talking flavor. It is also sweet for your health.

- Sweeten your antioxidant defenses – The trace minerals in maple syrup are an essential component for energy production and antioxidant defence.
- Be sweet to your heart – Maple syrup protects the health of your heart. It can decrease sclerosis, protect the inner lining of blood vessels and raise the levels of the 'good' cholesterol.
- Support for your immune system — Maple syrup is rich in zinc and manganese both of which are important allies in the immune system. Regular intake of maple syrup acts as an immuno-stimulant and strengthens the body's immune response.
- Special benefits for men - This sweet nectar provides superior reproductive health by protecting the prostate gland. It also participates in the production of sex hormones, thus helping to maintain reproductive health.

Honey: Aah! The nectar of God.

It is a veritable store house of minerals & vitamins.

Honey contains Sugar like glucose and fructose and minerals like magnesium, potassium, calcium, sodium chlorine, sulphur, iron and phosphate.

It contains vitamins B1, B2, C, B6, B5 and B3 besides also having copper, iodine, and zinc and several kinds of hormones. This dynamo of a sweetener has powerful antimicrobial properties, which can soothe raw tissues. Its natural anti- inflammatory effect and its potency to kill viruses, bacteria, and fungus make it a must have, must use in every household.

Taking Honey as a sweetener in the exotic blends can allay seasonal allergies, soothe the inner wall of stomach, treat stomach ulcers & act as a natural antiseptic.

Anti-ageing Exotic Blends

Rock Candy: A simple derivative of Sugar cane juice available in chunky pieces and larger than plain Sugar. A good sweetener to use as it soothes the throat, relieving irritation, dry cough and hoarseness.

Also called misri and used in many of the blends.

Another variety available is made from molasses of Palm juice extract. It is called PALM CANDY and has therapeutic properties of relieving cough and cold, recovers one from physical exhaustion & assists in sleep. Its regular intake keeps the body strong.

It can be substituted for Rock Candy in a blend.

Jaggery: It is another derivative of Sugar cane juice. It is a healthier sweetener to consume.

Jaggery is less refined than crystal Sugar and is available in forms which have been made without adding chemicals. It is preferable to procure unsulphured jaggery, with the other options like jaggery made from date palm.

A small piece taken according to taste would suffice to lend your favorite blend a unique taste and flavor.

CHAPTER 7
Your Exotic Blends: Therapeutic Energizing and Anti-ageing

3 FLAVOURS INFUSION

Ingredients	Qty.
Dried spearmint	– ½ teaspoon
Lemon verbena leaves	– 10 fresh
Lemon grass	– 1 Long stalk
Lemon juice	– 1 teaspoon
Honey or Maple syrup	– ½ teaspoon
Water	– 200 ml

Preparation: Pluck fresh lemon verbena leaves and a thick stalk of lemon grass from the herbs garden. Wash and chop them finely.

How to create: Take water in a pan and allow it to boil. Add spearmint, chopped lemon verbena leaves and lemon grass to it. Allow the water to simmer slowly on the flame for 3-5 minutes. After this turn off the flame.

Keep it covered for a while and pour it in a cup, passing it through a sieve. Add the sweetener of your choice. Stir it in and enjoy the infusion.

BENEFITS

Anti-ageing: Three excellent herbs to enhance well being.

The maple syrup works wonders for the heart and protects blood vessels as well.

For men, this blend helps in maintaining the reproductive organs. Lemon verbena is the herb for anti-ageing, as it has the ability to assist in breaking down cellulite and to exert a soothing, healing and toning effect on the skin.

ACID NEUTRALIZER

Ingredients	Qty.
Bishop's seeds	– 1/3 teaspoon
Dried mint leaves	– 1 teaspoon
Or	
Fresh mint	– 20 leaves
Fresh dates	– 3 pieces
Water	– 400 ml

Preparation: Wash dates and the fresh mint leaves properly.

How to create: Take 400 ml water in a pan. Add all the ingredients in water. Boil bishop's seeds and mint and dates for 5-8 minutes till dates soften. Take out dates separately, de-seed them and mash the flesh. Sieve the blend. Add the mashed dates back to the water and boil it again. Pour it into a cup. Drink while eating the dates.

BENEFITS

Energizing: Dates – the 'Crown of sweets' is an ideal food which is easy to digest. An exhausted body gains renewed vigour within half an hour of taking it. Dates are the best stimulant for muscles. Men of all ages can consume them to increase their muscular capacity and stamina.

Therapeutic: At times, when food is not digested properly leading to acidity or gastritis, this blend provides an alkaline effect. The acid Neutralizer Blend is helpful when a person is suffering from acidity, hyperacidity and gastric problems.

AGILE – PARSLEY

Ingredients	Qty.
Fresh parsley sprigs	– 50 grams
Fresh mint leaves	– 20 leaves
Fresh ginger rhizome	– Thin slice
Honey	– 1 teaspoon
Lemon juice	– 1 tablespoon
Water	– 200 ml

Preparation: Wash parsley and mint leaves properly. Peel off ginger and wash it. Make a paste of parsley, mint and ginger.

How to create: Boil water in a pan. Remove it from the flame and add paste of parsley, mint and ginger. Cover the pan and allow the ingredients to steep in the water. Squeeze out the juice of the lemon and add honey to it. Stir well. Add this sweet lemony juice to the infusion and mix it well. Sieve it in a glass and cool it to enjoy the blend.

Optional: This blend can also be taken warm.

BENEFITS

Anti-ageing: Parsley is rich in volatile oils and flavonoids, which functions as antioxidants. It is an excellent source of vitamin C, which renders dangerous free radicals harmless in all water soluble areas of the body.

This underestimated herb also contains beta carotene, strengthening your immune system.

Halt premature ageing; keep good health and strong immunity. In two words - REMAIN AGILE with this blend.

ALMOFIGS

Ingredients	Qty.
Figs	– 2 pieces
Almonds (Mamra variety preferable)	– 6 pieces
Water	– 200 ml

Preparation: Wash and soak figs and almonds overnight. Chop the figs finely before using. Peel the almonds and keep aside.

How to create: Boil 200 ml water in a pan. When water starts boiling add the soaked figs with the water in which they were soaked. Cover the pan and put off the flame.

Pour the infusion into a cup. No sweetener is required.

Enjoy the almonds, chewing them well into creamy consistency while drinking the delicious blend.

BENEFITS

Anti-ageing: Almonds are the 'King of nuts'. They are brimming with calcium, essential fatty acids (EFA's) and a host of nutro–chemicals, which exert a synergic action in maintaining the smooth functioning and vitality of the brain, in strengthening the muscles and in prolonging life.

ANTIOXIDANT FOUNTAIN

Ingredients	Qty.
Dried red apple	– 1 tablespoon
or Freshly grated red apple	– 2 tablespoon
Munakkas	– 2 pieces
Water	– 200 ml

Preparation: Wash *munakkas* and chop them. Take a fresh red apple and grate the required quantity.

How to create: Boil water in a pan. Add chopped munakkas with their seeds. Allow water to simmer for 2-3 minutes. Take the chopped munakkas out with a spoon and put them in a cup. Add grated red apple to the simmering water and turn off the flame. Cover the pan. Let it steep for 5 minutes. Strain it in the cup containing munakkas.

Drink the fine tasting blend while picking munakkas to savour them along with their benefits.

BENEFITS

Anti-ageing cum Energizing: The name says it all. The incredibly potent mix of the above two ingredients make this blend a 'must have' for all in the family.

Give it to children primarily for its active components, which make better bones, healthy gums and teeth. For women the phytonutrients in this blend provides oestrogen in a natural way keeping the glandular system balanced.

APHRODISIAC

Ingredients	Qty.
Saffron	– ¼ teaspoon
Fresh ginger rhizome	– 2 inches
Clear honey	– 2 teaspoon
Water	– 200 ml

Preparation: Peel and wash ginger. Shred ginger in julienne and fold it in clear organic honey. Leave it in a small jar for 24 hours and use it after that.

How to create: To make this blend, dissolve saffron in 50 ml water. Boil rest of the 150 ml water. Add the water containing saffron to this and boil it again.

Take out 1 teaspoon (heaped) honeyed-ginger and put it in a cup. Pour the contents from the pan on the honeyed-ginger and stir well. Sieve, sip and savour.

BENEFITS

Anti-ageing: An 'Out of this world' blend which gives all the senses a tingling feeling.

Greek mythology associates saffron with fertility and is considered as an excellent stimulant. Ginger has strong antioxidant activity with nutrients that keep your mood elated.

APRICARDO

Ingredients	Qty.
Dry apricots	– 4 pieces
Green cardamom	– 1 piece
Powdered spearmint	– A pinch
Water	– 200 ml

Preparation: Soak apricots overnight in more than one cup of water. Strain the soaked apricots and keep water for the blend. De-seed and mash the apricots well. Put these in your cup and keep them aside.

How to create: Boil the water in which the apricots were soaked. Add crushed green cardamom to it. Add a pinch of spearmint. Put off the flame and allow it to steep for 5 minutes. Strain & pour the blend over mashed apricots and stir well mixing in their sweetness.

Sip and enjoy the crunch of the soft apricots.

BENEFITS

Energizing: You smell from the nose and digest in the stomach. This blend affects both. The aroma of the blend lifts you higher, the taste lingers and the stomach improves.

The dry apricot itself is a fruit bursting with minerals and vitamins to recharge the body.

BARLEY MAGIC

Ingredients	Qty.
Barley grains	– ½ cup
Rock candy	– ½ teaspoon
Lemon for garnishing	– 1 wedge
Water	– 250 ml

Preparation: Wash the barley grains and soak overnight in 250 ml of water.

How to create: Boil the barley grains only once in water in which it was soaked. Strain the blend in a glass and add rock candy. Stir it well. Decorate it with a wedge of lemon. Drink it hot in winters and chill it in summers.

BENEFITS

Anti-ageing: The barley grain has a matrix of nutrients bound up in it. These multifunctional antioxidants affect your body dynamically keeping the inner vitals functioning at the highest level. Taking this blend ensures the inclusion of this grain in your dietary pattern. The barley cereal weaves its magic by rejuvenating and healing the digestive system.

BLESSED YOUTH

Ingredients	Qty.
Red skinned potato	– 2 pieces
Fresh ginger Rhizome	– ¼ teaspoon - grated
Rock candy	– ½ teaspoon
Water	– 200 ml

Preparation: Wash the potatoes well but do not peel them. Scoop out the eyes of potatoes and slice them round. Soak them in 200 ml of water. Add grated ginger and rock candy to it. Cover and leave it overnight in the refrigerator in summers and at room temperature in winters.

How to create: Strain the fluid and warm it on slow flame. Do not boil it. Pour in a cup and sip it slowly.

BENEFITS

Anti-ageing: Potatoes contain unique tuber storage proteins, which exhibit activity against free radicals protecting the body against the ravages of the environment, toxins, synthetic chemicals, smoke and ageing.

BONE STRENGTHENER

Ingredients	Qty.
Red apple	– ¼ of an apple Can be of any variety - Himalayan or Fujian
Figs	– 2 pieces
Water	– 250 ml

Preparation: Wash the apple and grate it. Wash the figs thoroughly removing all dirt and straw from it and chop it finely.

How to create: Put water in a pan with the grated apple and chopped figs. Cover the pan. Boil and simmer for two minutes. Sweetening is not required.

Do not strain it. Pour the blend in a glass. Drink and relish while eating the figs.

The drink can be enjoyed both hot or cold.

BENEFITS

Anti-ageing: Apple and its peel provide antioxidants in the most fragrant and sweety way.

This blend provides calcium, increases bone density and its mineral contents make it a superb addition to the diet.

CHILDREN'S FAVORITE

Ingredients	Qty.
Fresh lemon grass	– 6-8 stalks of 4" length
Lemon juice	– 1 tablespoon
Rock candy	– 1 teaspoon
Water	– 250 ml

How to create: Wash the freshly cut lemon grass well and chop the stalks. Put them in a pan. Add water in the pan and allow it to boil. Turn off the flame. Let the leaves steep in it for at least 10 minutes.

Squeeze in juice of one whole lemon and stir in rock candy. Strain and pour the blend in a cup and sip it warm.

Optional: You can also chill it and take it as an ice-tea in summers.

BENEFITS

Energizing: The Vitamin C in lemon helped Hillary in scaling the Mt. Everest, the highest peak in the world. This blend would take your child to his health's peak.

The tangy flavour and the potency of lemon grass for improving digestion makes it a favourite amongst the kids.

Note : You can also use dried lemon grass herb of equal quantity.

CIRCULATION ACCELERATOR

Ingredients	Qty.
Corn on the cob with silk threads	– 1 piece
Fresh ginger juice	– 4 drops
Rock candy	– ½ teaspoon
Water	– 200 ml

Preparation: Remove husk from the corn cob taking care to protect the silk threads. Do not let them fall out. Separate them from the husk and keep them aside.

How to create: Boil water in a pan. Add all the silk threads of the corn cob. Cover the pan and simmer on slow flame and cook it for 5 minutes.

Strain the blend in a cup and add freshly extracted ginger juice. Sweeten with rock candy and drink it warm.

BENEFITS

Anti-ageing: The kidneys are one of the most vital organs of the body. This blend works on kidneys stimulating them to function better.

Therapeutic: The corn silk threads have a particular property of resolving the urinary tract infections, bladder disorders and even kidney stones. Regular intake of this blend prevents such disorder and keeps the urinary tract healthy.

CURRY BLEND

Ingredients	Qty.
Tender curry leaves	– 25 (approx.)
Rock candy	– 1 teaspoon
Lemon	– 1 juiced
Water	– 250 ml

How to create: Wash & chop curry leaves and put them in a pan with 250 ml water and bring it to a boil. Allow the mix to simmer for a while. Add rock candy and stir. Do not strain it. Pour it in your glass and add juice of one lemon to it. Stir it. You can take it cool or even warm according to your wish and desire.

BENEFITS

Anti-ageing: Curry leaves purify blood and detoxify the body naturally. Vitamin C present in lemon is a versatile and powerful antioxidant that has shown the ability to even stop the growth of HIV, the AIDS virus in test tubes.

Therapeutic: Dysentery is a common disease among kids during rainy season primarily due to eating outside. Taking curry blend is helpful under such circumstances. Repeat it every 3 hours for fast relief.

DIABETES CURE

Ingredients	Qty.
Fenugreek seeds	– 1 teaspoon
Black pepper corns	– 5 pieces - crushed
Rock candy	– ½ teaspoon
Water	– 250 ml

How to create: Boil water in a pan. Add fenugreek seeds and crushed pepper corns once water starts boiling. Cover the pan and let water simmer for 2-3 minutes. Put off the flame without removing the pan cover to make the decoction more beneficial. Strain and pour the blend in a cup and add rock candy to sweeten it. Stir well and sip it for multiple advantages.

BENEFITS

Therapeutic: This distinctive blend can lower the level of blood sugar, acts on the liver and improves metabolism.

The magic seeds of fenugreek are an effective nutritional supplement with the ability to induce the production of insulin when blood sugar levels are elevated.

The pepper corns stimulate the taste buds and send an alert to the stomach to increase hydrochloric acid secretion thereby, increasing the metabolic rate.

Cheers to your health!

DISTINCT AFTER TASTE

Ingredients	Qty.
Fresh mint leaves	– 20 leaves
Cinnamon	– ¾ stick
Bay leaf	– ½ leaf
Fresh ginger rhizome	– ¼ inch
Rock candy	– 1 teaspoon
Water	– 200 ml

Preparation: Wash and chop the mint leaves. Wash cinnamon stick and bay leaf in running water. Peel the ginger and chop it very finely. Crush bay leaf and cinnamon.

How to create: Add all the above ingredients in 200 ml of boiling water. Let it simmer for a minute or so in a covered pan. Switch off the flame and let it cool for a while. Strain and pour it in a cup, stirring in the sweetener.

BENEFITS: Lift up the soul with the dawn of the day by brewing this blend. It will give the rest of the day the distinction it deserves.

Anti-ageing: A clean and healthy intestine is vital for a youthful capacity to function. Mint destroys the most harmful bacteria & fungi in the digestive tract.

Bay leaf helps in keeping the intestines healthy. The fresh ginger rhizome being a natural antibiotic further completes the task.

Therapeutic: Bay leaf provides warmth to the body and is highly effective for cold. Bay leaf blend aids in migraine therapy.

EARLY DAY STIMULANT

Ingredients	Qty.
Chamomile flowers	– ½ teaspoon
Lemon grass	– 1 long stalk
Lemon juice	– 1 teaspoon
Honey or Rock candy	– ½ teaspoon – to taste
Water	– 200 ml

Preparation: Cut fresh lemon grass stalk from the pot. Snip it from the bottom as the bottom is thick and juicy to make the infusion aromatic. Wash off the mud & grime and chop it finely.

How to create: Put lemon grass in a pan containing the specified quantity of water and boil it for 2-3 minutes. Add dried chamomile flowers to it. Cover the pan and put off the flame. Allow it to steep for 10 minutes.

Strain the exquisite herbal concoction into a cup. Add lemon juice as well as sweetener of your choice.

Stir and drink while inhaling the nerve relaxing aroma.

BENEFITS: This blend prepares you for the day. It has a stimulating effect on the body and senses. A choice of sweetener gives the option of choosing the benefits.

Therapeutic: The mix of lemon juice and lemon grass cleanses the intestinal tract of debris. It clears up the mucous leaving you feeling brand new.

Honey soothes the stomach wall, treats stomach ulcers & acts as a natural antiseptic.

Rock candy removes dry cough and hoarseness.

Anti-ageing Exotic Blends

ENERGIZE ME

Ingredients	Qty.
Prunes	– 2 pieces
Green cardamom	– 1 piece
Water	– 200 ml

Preparation: Soak prunes overnight in 200 ml water. Make a fine powder of green cardamom seeds. Take out prunes from water, chop them and put them in a glass. Keep the soaking water aside.

How to create: Taking a pan heat the water in which prunes were soaked and sprinkle green cardamom powder in it. Cover the pan and turn off the flame when water is hot. Pour it on the chopped prunes in the glass and chill it before drinking. No need to add any sweetener.

Optional: The blend can also be taken warm.

BENEFITS

Energizing: The prune blend energizes for the day ahead. Prunes are loaded with antioxidants. They are good for nerves due to their high Phosphorous content. Cardamom is a wonderful mouth freshener. It refreshes the digestion process also by aiding it and assisting in the release of energy from food which is eaten.

EVENING UNWIND

Ingredients	Qty.
Dried rose petals	– 1 tablespoon
Saffron	– ¼ teaspoon
Maple syrup	– ¼ teaspoon
Water	– 250 ml

Preparation: Collect fresh, fragrant and multicoloured rose petals from the garden. Dry them in shade and cover to protect them from dust. Keep them in an air tight jar to make the evening unwind blend.

How to create: Boil water in a pan for a minute before adding any ingredients to it. Add rose-petals and saffron to it. Turn the flame off and cover the pan for 15 minutes to steep it well. Saffron will leave behind a nice attractive colour. Add maple syrup and stir it. Strain this aromatic blend in a cup. Put 3 or 4 threads of saffron to float on the blend.

Optional: This blend can also be taken cold in a glass.

"You've been working awfully hard lately. If you need a little fresh air and sunshine, you can go to www.fresh-air-and-sunshine.com"

BENEFITS

Dried rose petals are available in the market from provisional stores. Fresh red rose petals with soft fragrance can also be picked up from the personal garden.

Anti-ageing: The maple syrup strengthens the antioxidant defences and acts as an immuno–stimulant.

It protects Prostate gland of men and participates in the production of sex hormones, thereby, helping to maintain reproductive health.

Therapeutic: This infusion has a mild sedating effect. The essence of the rose flower has a positive influence on the entire well being.

EXPAND YOUR BREATH

Ingredients	Qty.
Fresh eucalyptus leaves	– 3 pieces
Honey	– ½ teaspoon
Water	– 200 ml

Preparation: Collect small fresh leaves of the eucalyptus tree and break them into halves. Wash them well.

How to create: Take water in a pan and boil it. Add eucalyptus leaves to the boiling water.

Allow the water to simmer for 5 minutes in a covered pan. Strain it into a cup and add honey. Stir well with a spoon.

Taking the blend steaming hot is advisable for better results. Taking the blend cold or lukewarm should be avoided.

BENEFITS

Anti-ageing: The eucalyptus leaves increase the capacity of lungs to breath by dissolving the mucus. It removes mucus from the entire respiratory tract, cleaning the passage to give greater stamina.

Therapeutic: The healing effect of the blend is convincing from the first sip itself.

It is curative for lung disorders, cold and sore throats. It would open up the nasal passages when the hot steam from the cup is inhaled, helping in cases of mild to moderate snoring.

GENTLE DETOX

Ingredients	Qty.
Dried tarragon herb	– 1 teaspoon
Cloves	– 2 pieces
Dates	– 2 pieces
Ginger	– ¼ teaspoon
Water	– 200 ml

Preparation: Pound the cloves. Wash & de-seed the dates and chop them.

Wash, peel and shred the ginger.

How to create: Boil water in a pan. Add tarragon, cloves and the shredded ginger. Add de-seeded and chopped dates to the water. Boil the water 2-3 times. Turn off the flame.

Keep the pan covered and allow the ingredients to steep. Mash dates well with a spoon to lend their taste to the blend. Strain and partake.

BENEFITS

Anti-ageing: Tarragon aids in digestion and accelerates the process of detoxifying the body of its toxic waste. A cleansed system retains its efficiency. This blend does that for you.

Cloves form a protective shield from environmental pollutants.

Energizing: Tarragon, is a herb which with its multiple benefits assists in fighting fatigue and calming down the nerves.

Dates surpass other fruits in the sheer variety of their constituents. They contain stimulants that strengthen the muscles.

HEALTH CONFIGURATION

Ingredients	Qty.
Fresh radish leaves	– 10 pieces
Lemon juice	– 1 teaspoon
Black salt	– ¼ teaspoon
Water	– 200 ml

Preparation: Select clean and fresh leaves of radish. Wash them well and chop finely. Squeeze lemon and keep the juice aside.

How to create: Take water in a pan and boil it. Add chopped radish leaves. Cover the pan and allow it to simmer on minimum flame for five minutes. Strain it in a cup. Add the freshly squeezed lemon juice and black salt. Stir well to mix in the ingredients. Serve warm.

BENEFITS

Anti-ageing: The liver being the gland responsible for a clean blood stream and good metabolism, it is the gland in focus for retaining youth.

Therapeutic: Taking the health configuration aids in digesting & assimilating fats in the diet. It eases bile flow and assists in breaking down gall bladder stones. This blend hits the bull's eye. It rejuvenates the liver, raises the metabolism, aids in detoxifying the body of toxic matter and synthetic chemicals.

HONEYED CHLOROPHYLL

Ingredients	Qty.
Potato	– 1 piece, medium size (organic)
Fresh Mint	– 20 leaves
Organic honey	– ½ teaspoon
Water	– 200 ml

Preparation: Wash mint leaves and a potato well under running water. Scoop out the eyes of potato and wash it again. Cut potatoes into large squares to prepare for juicing.

How to create: Take the potato and mint leaves and juice them together. Keep the freshly extracted juice aside in a glass.

Boil water in a pan and then cool it slightly. Add honey to it and stir it well. Add potato and mint juice to it. Stir again.

Drink it immediately to get full nutritional content.

BENEFITS

Anti-ageing: Fresh potato juice is like ambrosia for the human body. It's vitamin C, vitamin B6, copper, potassium and manganese content promotes inner wellbeing. The phytonutrients in potato and mint are essential for the formation of all new cells in the body. Honey contains several kinds of hormones that assist in maintaining the hormonal balance of the body.

Therapeutic: Potato juice is an alkaliser par excellence. It neutralizes acidity and builds up the alkaline reserve. Honey and mint, both prevent growth of harmful microbes in your body.

The dark green aromatic herb called Mint is an internal cleanser. In hot weather it refreshes and delightfully cools the body system.

IMMUNITY RAISER

Ingredients	Qty.
Holy basil	– 15 to 20 leaves
Pepper corns	– 4 pieces
Dry grounded ginger	– ¼ teaspoon
Honey	– ½ teaspoon
Water	– 200 ml

Preparation: Wash the holy basil leaves thoroughly under running water and chop them. Coarsely crush the pepper corns.

How to create: Take finely chopped holy basil leaves and add them to a pan containing 200 ml water. Put it on flame to boil. Add coarsely crushed pepper corns and dry ginger powder to it. Boil it for 2 to 3 minutes. Strain it in a cup and stir in the honey.

BENEFITS:

Tip: Pluck holy basil leaves before sun set.

Anti-ageing: Holy basil leaves are a nerve tonic and help sharpen memory. An active nervous system with clear and vibrant signals keeps you young and fit.

Energizing: Holy basil leaves are regarded as an adaptogen or anti-stress agent. This blend provides you significant protection against stress. Honey being a sweetener easily assimilated, it recharges your body by reaching the blood stream quickly.

Therapeutic: It raises the immunity level and resistance to pollutants. Its regular intake has marvelous effects on children.

INFUSE YOUR IMMUNITY

Ingredients	Qty.
Cinnamon	– 1 ½" stick
Black cumin seeds	– ½ teaspoon
Honey	– ½ teaspoon
Water	– 200 ml

Preparation: Wash cinnamon stick and break it in to small pieces.

How to create: Take water in a pan and boil it. Add pounded cinnamon in the boiling water with black cumin seeds. Cover the pan and allow it to boil for 2 minutes. Turn off the flame. Keep it covered for a while to allow the infusion of cinnamon and black cumin seeds to blend well. Pour honey in a cup and strain the infusion into it. Stir to mix in the honey.

BENEFITS:

Anti-ageing: These two nutrient dense spices do wonders for your health. Black cumin has been used by millions of people for its immunity enhancing properties. It stimulates the bone marrow and immune cells to function better.

When combined with the 'King of spice,' cinnamon, the blend becomes anti-ageing in nature. Cinnamon boosts cognitive function and memory capacity.

KEEP THE COLD AWAY

Ingredients	Qty.
Fresh Sweet basil	– 20 fresh leaves
Rock candy	– ½ teaspoon
Lemon	– ½ juiced
Water	– 250 ml

Preparation: Wash and chop sweet basil leaves.

How to create: Add sweet basil leaves to 250 ml of water in a pan. Boil till the water reduces to 150 ml or 1 cup. Strain your blend. Add rock candy and squeeze half a lemon. Mix well and sip.

BENEFITS:

Therapeutic: Aromatic sweet basil leaves check the sputum and are beneficial in common cold, cough and other respiratory and chest discomforts.

Lemon juice has the power to destroy toxins in the body and eliminate intestinal worms.

A ripe lemon is a good appetizer. Lemon juice stimulates the flow of saliva and gastric juices.

KEEP YOU SLIM BLEND

Ingredients	Qty.
Pepper corns	– 4 pieces
Sultanas	– 6 pieces
Fresh thyme or Dried	– 2 twigs – 1 teaspoon
Water	– 450 ml

Preparation: Wash and chop fresh thyme leaves. Slice washed sultanas.

How to create: Boil water in a pan. Crush the pepper corns to make a coarse powder and add them to water. Cover the pan and simmer for 2 minutes. Then add thyme and again simmer for 2 minutes keeping the pan covered. Add sliced sultanas. Simmer till sultanas are soft enough to be mashed and have lent sweetness to the blend. Strain and pour this exotic blend into your large designer glasses and savour.

Note: Serves 2

BENEFITS

Anti-ageing: Sultanas are sundekhani raisins taking their place as an antioxidant-rich fruit. They also contain the trace mineral Boron vital for women for better bone health.

Black pepper has impressive antioxidant and antibacterial effects. The outer layer of the peppercorn stimulates the breakdown of fat cells, keeping you slim.

LIFE FORCE

Ingredients	Qty.
Poppy seeds	– 1 tablespoon
Black peppercorns	– 2 pieces
Green cardamom	– Inner pods of 1 large piece
Mint leaves	– 2 small sprigs
Rock candy	– 1 teaspoon
Water	– 220 ml (including soaking water) at room temperature

Preparation: Put poppy seeds, peppercorns and cardamom pods in a cup with minimum water. Soak them overnight. Wash and chop the mint leaves.

How to create: In the morning add rock candy to the above ingredients. Make a paste of the mixture without draining water in which it was soaked. Put this paste in a glass, pour in the rest of the water and stir in well to make your morning health drink ready.

Cool it for a while in the refrigerator to make it more refreshing. Decorate the blend before serving with mint leaves.

BENEFITS

Anti-ageing: This life giving blend has bee prepared without heating it, thereby packing in all the nutrients of the ingredients unaltered as Nature intended.

Therapeutic: The poppy seeds have a remarkable sedating property. They also keep the blood flow healthy by providing the coagulant factor.

LIME 'N' LEMONY

Ingredients	Qty.
Dried orange rind	– ½ teaspoon
Fresh lemon rind	– ¼ rind of the whole lemon
Fresh lemon grass	– 6 stalks of 4" length
Rock candy	– 1 teaspoon
Water	– 450 ml

Preparation: During the orange season take the peels of oranges and dry them in semi shade. Grind them and preserve in an air tight jar.

Take a yellow lemon having thin peel. Wash it well and wipe dry. Take a sharp knife and start cutting the peel from one side of the lemon. Keep peeling round the lemon to take ¼th of the whole lemon. Chop the rind into small pieces.

How to create: Boil 450 ml water in a pan. Add all the ingredients to the boiling water and turn off the flame. Cover the pan and allow the citrus flavours to get steeped (do not boil after adding the ingredients). Strain, add rock candy and stir to sweeten it. Pour half the blend in a glass or cup and enjoy it hot. Take the remaining half and chill it well to have the taste of a cool blend.

BENEFITS

Energizing: Enjoy the citrus blend and get maximum vitamin C. The orange and lemon rind provides nutrients, which raises your energy levels.

Their health promoting properties match perfectly with those required by the body to keep it going like a dynamo. The lemon rind is a rich source of vitamin P and strengthens the entire arterial system. It consequently improves the blood circulation in the body.

The orange rind is desirably aromatic and refreshing.

MINT & THYME

Ingredients	Qty.
Fresh Mint	– 20 leaves
Dried thyme	– ½ teaspoon
Rose hips	– 5 pieces
Honey	– ½ teaspoon
Water	– 200 ml

Preparation: Wash the mint leaves and rose hips thoroughly.

How to create: Take 200 ml water in a pan. Add mint leaves, thyme and rose hips to the water. Boil the three together. Strain it into a cup and stir in honey for sweetening.

Sip it hot while inhaling its steam. It will enhance the effect.

BENEFITS

Anti-ageing: Thyme herb has significant antioxident capacity to protect cellular membranes and is highly effective in delaying brain cells from ageing.

Rose hips themselves are bursting with vitamins A, B3, C, D and E.

Therapeutic: Infusion of mint, thyme and rose hips helps in common cold & hay fever.

One should get into the bed and cover himself properly after drinking the infusion. It will give sound sleep.

MINTY DATES

Ingredients	Qty.
Fresh mint	– 30 leaves
Fresh ginger rhizome	– ½ inch piece
Dates	– 2 pieces
Water	– 200 ml

Preparation: Pick clean leaves of fresh mint. Wash and chop them coarsely. Wash, peel and grate ginger. Wash dates and de-seed them and remove the top to shred them.

How to create: Boil water in a pan. Add mint leaves to the boiling water. Also add grated ginger and shredded dates to the boiling water. Turn off the flame and keep the pan covered for 5 minutes. Stir well to mash dates and ginger.

To relish dates, ginger & mint, do not strain them. Just, pour the blend in a cup, enjoy it while sipping and chewing.

BENEFITS

The wonderful aroma, great taste and the healing power of mint brings to your cup a blend of pleasure and nutrition.

Anti-ageing: Dates contain oil, calcium, sulphur, iron, potassium, phosphorous, manganese, copper and magnesium. In other words, a date everyday is a minimum of a balanced and healthy diet. With two in this blend – the effect is doubled.

Therapeutic: Dates being rich in calcium help strengthen the bones. When calcium content in the body decreases, children are affected with rickets and in adults bones become brittle and weak. These natural sweeteners counteract such effects.

MORNING T.E.A.SER

Ingredients	Qty.
Thai ginger	– A small piece
Dried Spearmint leaves	– ½ teaspoon
Maple syrup	– ½ teaspoon
Water	– 200 ml

Preparation: Wash, peel and chop Thai ginger.

How to create: Take water in a pan. Boil it with chopped Thai ginger. Add powdered spearmint a little later. Cover the pan to enhance the flavour of the blend. Simmer it for one minute and keep it covered for a while.

Strain this delightful blend of spearmint and Thai ginger into your cup stirring in maple syrup to top the taste and flavour.

BENEFITS

Energizing: Thai ginger is a powerhouse of a spice with multiple benefits and has been known since centuries for it's healing powers.

Its synergistic combination with mint leaves and maple syrup which contains components essential for energy production refreshes you every morning.

NATURAL FUEL

Ingredients	Qty.
Fresh parsley	– 1 bunch or 200 gm
Powdered nutmeg	– a pinch
Lemon juice	– 1 teaspoon
Rock candy	– ½ teaspoon
Water	– 200 ml

Preparation: Wash the parsley thoroughly along with its twigs.

How to create: Juice the parsley bunch in a glass and add a small pinch of finely powdered nutmeg. Add lemon juice and rock candy and stir it well.

Add water and stir it again. Take the blend empty stomach, either cool or slightly warm.

Note: The blend can be warmed by adding warm water. Avoid heating the juice.

BENEFITS

Anti-ageing: Flavonoids in parsley combine with highly reactive oxygen-containing molecules (oxygen radicals) and help in preventing oxygen-based damage to cells. In addition, extracts from parsley help in increasing the antioxidant capacity of blood.

Nutmeg's legendary ability of being an aphrodisiac makes this a highly recommended blend especially because of it's therapeutic benefit for premature ejaculation.

Energizing: While parsley is a wonderfully nutritious food with healing capacity, it's capacity is not appreciated well. Most people do not realise that this vegetable has more uses than just being a decorative garnish on restaurant meals. They do not know that parsley is actually a storehouse of nutrients which offers a delicious and vibrant taste.

NO MORE RICKETY BONES

Ingredients	Qty.
Celery	– 1 single stalk
Lemon grass	– 1 long stalk
Lemon juice	– 1 teaspoon
Honey	– ½ teaspoon
Water	– 250 ml

Preparation: Wash the celery and lemon grass well. Take care to clean the vein of the celery while washing.

Chop them finely.

How to create: Boil water in a pan. Add the finely chopped celery and lemon grass to it. Turn off the flame. Keep the pan covered for 8-10 minutes. Allow the flavour and the essential oils to be released in the blend. Strain and stir in the sweetener and lemon juice. Enjoy it chilled or warm according to your wish and the weather.

BENEFITS

Anti-ageing: Celery is abundant in Sodium.

Sodium is the 'Youth Element' since it keeps the joints flexible. It prevents calcium from depositing in joints or development of spurs.

Celery assists in the process of bone building as well.

Energizing: This blend contains active compounds that reduce stress hormones. They protect the blood vessels from constricting; keeping one relaxed and calm.

Therapeutic: Lemon grass, lemon juice, honey and celery - that's the power of four to boost immunity.

Taking this blend regularly activates the white blood cells - the defenders that target and eliminate potentially harmful cells.

OREGANO-ORANGE

Ingredients	Qty.
Fresh oregano	– 5 green stalks
or dried	½ teaspoon
Green cardamom	– 1 piece
Fresh orange juice	– 4 tablespoon
Black salt	– $1/3^{rd}$ teaspoon
Water	– $3/4^{th}$ cup

Preparation: Wash and chop fresh oregano stalks. Crush the cardamom to finely powdered form.

How to create: Keep pan on flame and boil water. Add powdered green cardamom to it and give 2-3 boils. Put off the flame and add chopped green stalks of oregano to the boiled water. Keep pan covered only for a minute. Cool it to room temperature before straining it into a glass. Add fresh orange juice and black salt. Stir well and sip this smooth blend. Remember not to boil or heat the oregano for long as it loses its flavour.

BENEFITS

Anti-ageing: Oregano has been shown to have over 42 times the antioxidant activity as apples and 30 times higher than potatoes. Vitamins are also antioxidants and play a crucial role in retarding the ageing process, keeping you young.

Energizing: This blend gets a particular zing from the orange juice which gives the zip required by you. All the juices of the body are stimulated while the senses of nose and tongue are pampered.

Therapeutic: The delightful flavour of oregano acts as an appetizer. This blend can be prescribed if your appetite is low. Savor this blend an hour before your lunch or before supper time and enjoy the meal to your maximum. Oregano leaves help digestive disorders and are considered a tonic for the stomach.

Note: Fresh green oregano can be purchased from vegetable vendors otherwise the dried variety can be used which is available throughout the year.

PEPCON INFUSION

Ingredients	Qty.
Liquorice	– 2-3 thin sticks
Dry coriander seeds	– 1 teaspoon
Black pepper corns	– 6 pieces
Rock candy	– to taste
Water	– 250 ml

Preparation: Pound the coriander seeds to break them into halves, making them more potent. Crush the liquorice to soft texture and coarsely pound the peppercorns.

How to create: Take one and half cup of water and add to it above mentioned ingredients except rock candy in a pan. Cover the pan. Let the water simmer on slow flame till the decoction is 2/3rd left. Strain the blend. Add rock candy to sweeten it and stir it well.

Drink it slowly to soothe your throat.

BENEFITS

Anti-ageing: Liquorice is one of the most potent herbs on the planet to increase the immunity of the body.

A strong immune system is a sure sign of youth with its ability to keep your body functioning at optimal levels.

Therapeutic: Person with throat pain and phlegm in the chest should sip a cup of this blend, steaming hot.

Take the blend again in the evening. When taken for three days it throws the mucous out and relieves the body.

PIC-ME-UP

Ingredients	Qty.
Dried rosemary leaves	– 1 teaspoon
Red apple	– ¼th of a whole fruit
Rock candy	– ½ teaspoon
Water	– 200 ml

Preparation: Take a washed red apple. Shred the apple with a grater to use a quarter of it for each person.

How to create: Take water in a pan and boil it. Add all the ingredients except rock candy and turn off the flame. Allow the above ingredients to steep in the water for 5 minutes. Strain it into a cup and stir in the rock candy.

Do not take very hot. Take just warm enough to soothe you. This sweet and fragrant blend is best taken in the morning or evening.

BENEFITS

Anti-ageing: Rosemary leaves stimulate the circulatory system. This blend is highly effective in combating hair loss as it promotes blood circulation in the scalp and growth of the hair follicles.

Therapeutic: Ooh! The exquisite herb good for migraine. It would pick you up when you are in a down mood and feeling low and depressed. Rosemary has a calming effect on the nerves. The natural sweetness of the apple aids in this process.

POTENT BENEFITS

Ingredients	Qty.
Powdered haritaki	– ½ teaspoon
Ginger juice	– ¼ teaspoon
Crushed green cardamom	– 1 piece
Honey	– ½ teaspoon
Water	– 200 ml

How to create: Boil water in a pan. Add to it powdered haritaki and crushed green cardamom. Cover the pan and turn off the flame. Allow it to steep for 5-10 minutes.

Strain it in a cup and add ginger juice and honey to it. Stir well and drink to your health.

BENEFITS

Anti-ageing: The combination of haritaki, ginger juice and cardamom is very potent for digestion and assimilation. Both being optimal is an excellent sign of good health and a vital body.

Haritaki itself is a rejuvenative fruit, which tones up the intestines.

POWER BUILDER

Ingredients	Qty.
Dried black currants	– 3 tablespoon
Almonds	– 20 pieces
Water	– 200 ml

Preparation: Soak the almonds overnight. Next morning peel off the almonds and chop them finely.

How to create: Take the chopped almonds and put them in a blender. Add black currants as well. Blend these two ingredients adding water in drops so that the mix becomes creamy. Add remaining water once the consistency becomes creamy. Pour it into a glass.

Chill the blend or add crushed ice to enjoy the drink.

BENEFITS

Anti-ageing: A living drink made from a dried fruit that is choc–a–block full of nutrients and the 'King of nuts'.

It is a rich source of proteins, carbohydrates, calcium and a host of minerals & vitamins essential for us on a daily basis.

Energizing: Build up your power day after day by drinking up this blend. Do not forget to share it with other family members as well. This power builder will load up the body's reserves whatever be the age.

REJUVENATOR

Ingredients	Qty.
Dried Turkish apricots	– 2 or 3 pieces
Fresh thyme	– 2 sprigs or dried 1 teaspoon
Almonds	– 4 pieces
Water	– 250 ml

Preparation: Soak almonds overnight. Peel almonds and chop them finely at the time of blend making. Soak Turkish apricots in 250 ml water (separately) overnight.

How to create: Boil apricots in it's soaking water. Add thyme for flavour, aroma and therapeutic benefits. Strain the infusion and take apricots out. Add them back to the blend after mashing them well. Add chopped almonds into the glass.

Chill the drink without straining it. Use a spoon to pick up the crunch along with sipping the blend.

Note : Keep the apricot soaking water in refrigerator in the morning till the time of usage.

BENEFITS

Turkish apricots are golden in colour and mildly tangy in taste which brings an exotic flavour to this infusion.

Anti-ageing: This blend is a potent health rejuvenator with calcium rich almonds and antioxidant rich Turkish apricots.

The almonds are nourishing foods that are easily assimilated. The chemico-nutrients present in them help the formation of new blood cells and play a major role in smooth functioning of the brain, nerves, bones, heart and liver. The apricots prevent premature ageing and protect the cells in the body.

SAFFRO-DIGEST

Ingredients	Qty.
Saffron	– ¼ teaspoon
Bishop's weed	– ¼ teaspoon
Powdered jaggery	– ½ teaspoon
Water	– 200 ml

How to create: Boil water in a pan. Add bishop's weed and saffron to it. Simmer the blend for a while keeping the pan covered. Turn off the flame.

Strain it into a cup and stir in the sweetener for satisfying your sweet tooth.

Take it warm.

BENEFITS

Therapeutic: Saffron is considered a superb stomach ailment remover and an antispasmodic.

It not only relieves your stomachache, it also relieves your tension, depression and sedates you mildly.

Adding bishop's weed to this blend is like adding 1 + 1 to make 11. The power of this blend increases exponentially by combining these two spices.

SEED POWER

Ingredients	Qty.
Fennel seeds	– 1 teaspoon
Bishop's weed	– ½ teaspoon
Caraway seeds	– ½ teaspoon
Lemon juice	– 1 tablespoon
Rock candy	– ½ teaspoon
Water	– 250 ml

How to create: Take water in a pan and boil it. Add fennel seeds, bishop's weed, & caraway seeds to water and give another boil. Turn off the flame. Allow it to steep for 5-6 minutes.

Strain it in a glass and add lemon juice. Stir in the rock candy and sip it warm.

Optional: This blend can also be taken cool.

BENEFITS

Anti-ageing: The caraway seeds, leaves and roots are considered useful in activating the secretions from glands. It is characterised as an excellent 'house cleaner' for the body.

Therapeutic: Phytonutrients in fennel seeds protect the liver from toxic chemical injury.

SMILES & SWEETS

Ingredients	Qty.
Fresh Thai ginger	– ½ inch piece
Dried chamomile flowers	– 1 teaspoon
Dried Raisins	– 6-8 pieces
Lemon juice	– ½ teaspoon
Water	– 400 ml

Preparation: Crush ginger with the roller pin. Wash and chop the raisins finely.

How to create: Boil water in a pan. Add crushed ginger and chamomile flowers to the boiling water. Boil for 10 minutes on minimum flame so that ginger and chamomile give their extract to the water. Strain and add chopped raisins. Leave it for 1-2 minutes for the raisins to soften. Mash raisins to lend proper sweetness. Add lemon juice and stir.

BENEFITS

Energizing: A hectic schedule of the entire day's work can make you mentally & physically fatigued. To calm yourself and your nerves, prepare 'Smiles & Sweets'. The chamomile flower will refresh the nervous system.

Thai ginger is a spicier version with strong antioxidant activity as well as an antidepressant that lifts your mood in minutes.

SOUL SOFTENER

Ingredients	Qty.
Liquorice	– 1 stick
Fresh holy basil	– 10 leaves
Fresh ginger rhizome	– ¼ inch piece
Honey	– 1 teaspoon
Water	– 250 ml

Preparation: Crush the liquorice stick. Wash the freshly plucked holy basil leaves. Peel ginger and crush along with the basil leaves.

How to create: Take water in a pan. Add all the above ingredients and boil them for 4-5 times on minimum flame. Strain into a cup. Add honey to the blend. Stir it well and consume it hot.

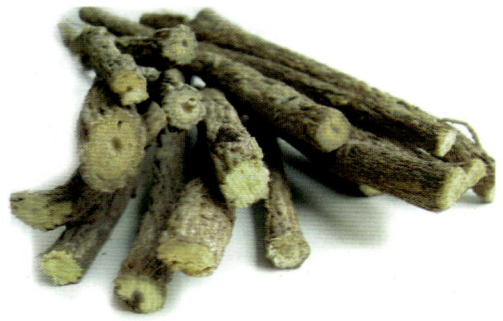

BENEFITS

Energizing: The natural sweetness of liquorice, the piquant taste of ginger, smooth honey and the flavour of holy basil all lift the spirit of the body.
Their individual energies combine to give you a blend that reaches deep within to do wondrous work of softening the soul.

SWEET & TANGY

Ingredients	Qty.
Dried lemon rind	– 4 pieces of ½ inch length
Honey	– 1 teaspoon
Water	– 200 ml

Preparation: Choose yellow lemons with thin peels from the market. Wash and wipe them dry. Take a sharp knife and start cutting the peel from one side of the lemon. Keep peeling round the lemon and you will get long curved strands. Chop them into small lengths of ½" each. Rub black salt to these lemon rinds.

Dry them in a semi sunny place, after covering them with a net. After they are dried, store them in a jar. They are now ready for use for the blends.

How to create: Boil water in a pan. Drop 4 strands of dried lemon rinds in the pan once water starts boiling. Turn the flame off. Allow it to steep for 5 minutes. Strain it into a cup and add honey to it. Take pleasure in this delectable fusion.

BENEFITS: The flavour of lemon and the sweetness of honey makes this blend a 'must-take'.

Energizing: Honey being a veritable store house of minerals, enzymes and natural hormones should be taken everyday.

This dynamo of a sweetener having the ability to kill viruses, bacteria and fungus keeps energy levels at a peak. Your body's defences are well stocked by taking this blend.

THE GREAT DIGESTIVE

Ingredients	Qty.
Dried thyme	– ½ teaspoon
Bishop's weed	– ¼ teaspoon
Fresh ginger rhizome	– ¼ inch piece
Honey	– ½ teaspoon
Water	– 200 ml

Preparation: Wash, peel and shred the fresh ginger.

How to create: Boil water in a pan. Add thyme, bishop's weed and shredded ginger to the boiling water. Cover the pan and turn off the flame. Let it steep for 5 minutes. Strain the infusion in a cup and add honey to it.

Inhale the aroma of thyme and taste the tangy mix of bishop's weed with ginger.

BENEFITS

Therapeutic: The essential oils in thyme decontaminate the intestines keeping them healthy and microbe free.

The combined effect of thyme and bishop's weed, which itself is a strong digestive herb doubles the potency of this blend.

The fresh ginger is a proven anti-emetic, anti-diarrhoeal spice that surpasses even pharmaceutical drugs.

Taste and health - the combination that compels you to take this infusion again and again.

THE SOOTHER

Ingredients	Qty.
Bishop's weed	– 1 teaspoon
Green cardamom	– 1 piece
Dry grounded ginger	– ½ teaspoon
Lemon juice	– 1 tablespoon
Rock candy	– To taste
Water	– 450 ml

Preparation: Crush the green cardamom along with pods.

How to create: Boil water in a pan with bishop's weed and powdered green cardamom. Add dried ginger. Give 3-4 boils keeping the pan well covered to retain its aroma. Turn off the flame keeping the pan covered for another 2 minutes.

Add one tablespoon lemon juice to it.

Strain & pour this aromatic blend in your cups.

Add rock candy according to taste and stir it well.

Note: Serves 2.

BENEFITS

Therapeutic: Cardamom is known as the Queen of spices. It is a key digestive element along with refreshing the breath and soothing the throat.

Bishop's weed is an anti-spasmodic beneficial for belching, flatulence and for treating colds, congestions and even stimulating the liver.

The multiple healing benefits of ginger enhance the soothing effect of this blend.

It is a proven anti-emetic, anti-motion sickness remedy, anti-depressant and anti-diarrhoeal with strong antioxidant activity.

TINGLE BERRY

Ingredients	Qty.
Indian gooseberry juice	– 25 ml
Grounded black pepper	– A pinch
Black salt	– ¼ teaspoon
Palm candy/ rock candy	– ½" cube / ½ teaspoon
Water	– 200 ml

Preparation: Take 2 large Indian gooseberries and wash them well. Sliver off any brown portions. You can juice them either by passing the flesh of the fruit through a juicer or taking the freshly grated, ground berries and putting them in a fine muslin cloth to squeeze the juice from them.

How to create: Warm 200 ml of water in a pan and keep it aside.

Pour the juice extracted from the Indian Gooseberries in a glass. Add black salt, ground pepper and palm candy. Stir well till the palm candy dissolves. Add lukewarm water and stir again. Take it empty stomach to benefit from its advantageous properties.

BENEFITS

Anti-ageing: The Indian gooseberry can virtually transform the human body. It is a rejuvenative par excellence. Palm candy adds to its inherent energy and this blend becomes your manna for anti-ageing.

Energizing: This blend caters to three tastes of the tongue: sweet, salty and the pungent. It replenishes and restores the electrolytic balance of the body. Take it everyday to remain fully charged.

Therapeutic: 'Tingle Berry' cleanses the toxic residue from the intestines. It builds resistance and fortifies against disorders of all kinds.

TISSUE GENERATOR

Ingredients	Qty.
Germinated wheat grain	– ½ cup
Green cardamom	– 1 piece
Black peppercorn	– 1 piece
Natural vanilla essence	– 1 drop
Maple syrup	– ½ teaspoon
Water	– 200 ml

Preparation: The preparation time for the wheat grain is 3 days. Soak good quality wheat grains in water. Strain the water after eight hours. Tie wheat grains in a clean and washed muslin cloth. Keep it in a covered utensil for 24 hours. Next keep it in a refrigerator for another 24 hours. Crush the green cardamom & the peppercorn into a powdered form.

How to create: In the morning, open the muslin cloth. Take the germinated wheat sprouts and soak them in water for half-an-hour. Strain this water and discard it. Put sprouts in the blender. Add black pepper and green cardamom. Grind it slowly by adding little water at a time to make it smooth and silky.

Once this consistency is reached, add in the maple syrup and blend it once again. Strain the blend. Add crushed ice or chill it to drink as your breakfast.

Note : The consistency of the blend should be milky.

BENEFITS
Anti-ageing: Wheat sprouts are good source of phytoestrogens – plant compounds that affect blood cholesterol levels, blood vessel elasticity, bone metabolism and many other cellular metabolic processes. With such a diverse range of function they are among the topmost foods to be included in the anti-ageing regimen. The benefits of the whole grain extend beyond this to deliver 100% health, even to children. The green cardamom being digestive and the black peppercorn having slimming properties, make this blend a super 'bonanza' drink to keep everyone in the family fully fit.

TOUTE BONNE

Ingredients	Qty.
Dried sage herb	– 1 tablespoon
or fresh sage	10 leaves
Sultanas	– 10
Water	– 200 ml

Preparation: Wash the sultanas well under running water by rubbing their crevices. Soak them in a glass of water and add dried sage herb. In case of fresh sage leaves do not soak them. In the morning, take out the sultanas from the water. Keep this water aside to be used later.

How to create: Wash fresh sage leaves and chop them. Put the sultanas and the chopped sage leaves in a blender and blend to a very fine texture by adding the water in which sultanas were soaked little by little. Once all the water has been used, pour the blend in a glass to enjoy it.

You can cool the blend if you desire.

BENEFITS

Anti-ageing: Sage is one of the herbs that keeps your brain cells young. It assists in maintaining the signal strength which gives you a youthful cognitive ability.

Energizing: Sultanas are a top source of phytonutrients, powering the human body by giving the most natural minerals and enzymes.

This Blend is a living food boosting your reserves.

Therapeutic: Sage herb, also known as 'toute bonne' which means 'all is well' says it all for keeping good health and vitality.

VANGOOSE BLEND

Ingredients	Qty.
Indian gooseberry juice	– 25 ml
Honey	– 1 teaspoon
Fresh ginger rhizome	– ½ inch piece
Fresh vanilla bean or	– ¼th piece
Natural vanilla Essence	– 2 drops
Water	– 80 ml

Among the purported health benefits of vanilla by ancient peoples was that it could act as an aphrodisiac. It has been prescribed by physicians to be drunk as an infusion for increasing the virility.
It has been claimed by a German physician in 1762 that 342 impotent men were changed into astonishing lovers from drinking vanilla decoctions.

Preparation: Take 2 large Indian gooseberries and wash them well. Sliver off any brown portions. You can juice them either by passing the flesh of the fruit through a juicer or taking the freshly grated, ground berries and putting them in a fine muslin cloth to squeeze the juice from them. Juice the ginger along with the gooseberries. If using fresh vanilla bean, chop it well.

How to create: Pour the juice extracted from the Indian gooseberries in a glass and add honey to it. Stir it well. Boil water in a pan along with the vanilla. Give it 2-3 times boils so as to extract the flavor of the spice. Keep it aside and cool it to room temperature. Strain the water and add it to the gooseberry juice. Stir it again to make the blend homogenous. Drink it daily in the morning.

BENEFITS

Anti-ageing: The Vitamin C content of the Indian Gooseberry provides mega nutrition for the cells. It increases the absorption of all other nutrients making your food, your medicine. You will find your skin glowing and your hair shining with the natural colour being maintained for years to come.

Energizing: Vanilla has antioxidant properties and is used to cure impotence, to exhilarate the brain, prevent sleep, to increase muscular energy and as an aphrodisiac.

Therapeutic: The combination of honey and Indian gooseberry juice becomes a powerful colon irrigator. Toxins retained for many years are also washed off making you squeaky clean from the inside out.

VITALIZE

Ingredients	Qty.
Java plum	– 2 pieces.
Fenugreek seeds	– 1 teaspoon
Rock candy	– To taste
Black salt	– A pinch
Water	– 200 ml

How to create: Chop rose apples with the seeds. Put them in the pan in 200ml water. Add Fenugreek seeds and allow the water to boil. Reduce the flame and simmer for 30 seconds while keeping the pan covered. Strain and add rock candy and salt to it. Stir well.

Sip it warm and enjoy the day with vigour and vitality.

BENEFITS

Energizing: After the relaxed night – one should be able to get up well rested, active and alert in the morning. If you feel lethargic and listless in the morning then vitalize is the blend for you.

Therapeutic: The dual combination of rose apple and fenugreek seeds does wonders on the liver enhancing the metabolic process.

WOMEN'S CHOICE

Ingredients	Qty.
Dried Thyme herb	– ½ teaspoon
Bishop's weed	– ½ teaspoon
Fresh ginger rhizome	– ½ inch piece
Clear honey	– 1 teaspoon
Water	– 200 ml

Preparation: Wash, peel and shred the fresh ginger.

How to create: Boil water in a pan and put thyme, bishop's weed and shredded ginger. Boil it twice. Turn off the flame, keeping pan covered for 5 minutes so as to steep the blend well.

Strain the infusion in a cup and add honey to increase the taste and benefit.

BENEFITS

Therapeutic: Thyme is a nutrient dense herb with a wide range of health supportive benefits, most important of which is that it prevents microbial contamination of the intestines. It keeps them healthy and microbe free.

The bishop's weed keeps the uterus healthy and is excellent for lactating mothers as it enhances the production of milk.

YELLOW MARVEL

Ingredients	Qty.
Fresh turmeric rhizome	– ½ inch piece
Light brown peppercorns	– 2 pieces
Raisins	– 8 pieces
Water	– 200 ml

Preparation: Pick out a few light brown peppercorns from the container of the black peppercorns and store them separately.

Wash turmeric rhizome and remove the skin. Wash it again and chop it finely. Pound the brown peppercorns.

How to create: Boil water in a pan. Add chopped turmeric and powdered peppercorns. Cover the pan and turn off the flame. Add the raisins and allow it to steep for few minutes. Pick out the raisins and keep them aside. Strain the yellow marvel blend in a cup.

Sip it warm while chewing the raisins.

BENEFITS

Anti-ageing: Turmeric rhizome is one of the marvellous spices given by Divine nature to mankind. Its main active ingredient curcumin, protects you from a host of age-related disorders. It lowers cholesterol, protects the liver from toxins, boosts stomach defences against acid, reduces blood sugar in diabetics and is a powerful antagonist of numerous cancer-causing agents.

Raisins and peppercorns protect the cells of the body from getting damaged, thereby, preventing premature ageing.

YOUR HEART'S BLEND

Ingredients	Qty.
Cinnamon powder	– ½ teaspoon
Rock candy or clear honey	– ½ teaspoon – ½ teaspoon
Water	– 250 ml

How to create: Boil 250 ml water in a pan and add cinnamon powder to it. Turn off the flame. Cover the pan and let it steep for 5-7 minutes.

Do not strain. Add rock candy or honey depending on your choice. Stir it well. Pour it in a glass. Chill this blend before taking it.

Optional: This blend can also be taken warm.

BENEFITS

Anti-ageing: Cinnamon spice has an anti-clogging effect on the arteries and veins, which keeps them young and supple. The clear, unclogged and flexible blood vessels keep you far younger than your age.

Therapeutic: Cinnamon is a blood regulator and helps in circulation of blood. This blend is excellent for heart patients and for general health. It is good for clearing up skin and acne. Lactating mothers should drink it for improving their baby's food.

CHAPTER 8
A to Z of Blends

HERBS TO HAVE OR PLANT IN HOUSE

Coriander	Parsley
Rosemary	Lemongrass
Fennel	Chamomile
Thyme	Mint
Bay leaf	Basil
	Tarragon

Anti-ageing Exotic Blends

YOUR SPICES AND SWEETENERS

Cinnamon
Liquorice
Fenugreek
Clove
Bay leaf
Black cumin
Saffron
Peppercorn
Cardamom

Honey
Maple syrup
Dates
Rock candy
Jaggery
Palm Candy

Instant benefits of these blends

- Healing & Curative effects
- Energizing impact – Keeps you charged for the day
- Invitation to the senses – Savour the flavours & aromas
- Bursting with antioxidants – Raising immunity levels
- Calming, soothing and strengthening the nerves
- Non-addictive
- Can be taken by children and adults alike

Tips to get maximum from your exotic blend

- Try a new combination which you never had earlier but feel could be effective for health
- When you read these recipes, bring out the potent flavour and sweeten it according to your own taste
- Use the blend for the whole family including kids to develop the habit of health-drinks
- Throw a party to introduce these delectable blends to your friends. Let it be the time to show your awareness towards health and you have adopted the most up to date knowledge available in the field of health in your lifestyle.

Your best snacks & tit-bits to go along with the blends

Weetabix – Whole Grain biscuits
McVities Digestive biscuits
Threptin biscuits
Pumpkin Seeds
Hazelnuts

Your blend – hot or chilled

- Never take very hot as it bruises the delicate & soft organs inside the body.
- Take warm drinks in the morning to cleanse the system and detoxify.
- Chill out with cool drinks. They are more refreshing & soothing when the mercury is soaring high. They keep the head cool and body relaxed.
- Chill your drink for a short time only so that it does not lose its life force. If it is kept for long, it would get oxidized by the surrounding air.

GLOSSARY

STRAIN – Pass the liquid through a strainer or sieve

CHILL – Cool the content in the refrigerator but not to freeze

GARNISH – A decoration (food) on the top

SIMMER – Keep a pan on minimum flame so that contents do not boil

MASH – Make into a soft mass by crushing the ingredient

CHOP – Cut into very small pieces

POUND – Hit with a heavy object to break into small pieces

CRUSH – Grind into a powder or a paste

SHRED – Cut into thin strips

GRATE – Reduce the food to small shreds by rubbing on a grater

STEEP – Allow the contents to remain in fluid

INFUSION – A drink prepared by soaking to extract the flavour and healing properties

Note: All recipes in this book are for a single portion unless wherever specified.

BIBLIOGRAPHY

1. Grandma's Remedies. Dignity Dialogue, 1997
2. H.K.Bakhru. Foods that Heal. Orient Paperbacks, 1991
3. H.K.Bakhru. Vitamins that Heal. Orient Paperbacks, 2005
4. Jean Carper. Food your miracle medicine. Simon & Schuster, 1995
5. Andi Clevely. The Herb Identifier. Lorenz Books, 1999
6. Bernard Jenson. Foods That Heal. Health & Harmony, 2001